Schöningh

EinFach Englisch

Unterrichtsmodell

Series Editor: Hans Kröger

L.A. Crash

by
Annika Heider
Iris Onderka

edited by
Ulrike Klein
Gabriele Kugler-Euerle

Einzelarbeit

Partnerarbeit

Gruppenarbeit

Unterrichtsgespräch

Schreibauftrag

Hausaufgabe

Audio-CD

filmische Präsentation

Projekt, offene Aufgabe

kreative Aufgabe

szenisches Spiel, Rollenspiel

Vorwort

Der Titel der Reihe **EinFach Englisch** verdeutlicht Zielsetzung und Programm zugleich. Einerseits soll Schülerinnen und Schülern auf einfache Art und Weise der Zugang zu klassischen, aber auch neuen literarischen Werken und Filmen ermöglicht werden, andererseits sollen Lehrerinnen und Lehrern in der Praxis erprobte Unterrichtsmodelle angeboten werden, die die wichtigsten methodisch-didaktischen Ansätze ihres Faches Englisch abdecken. Dabei sind die Modelle direkt, ohne langes Einlesen einsetzbar und stellen Unterrichtsarbeit konkret vor. Als besonders hilfreich für die Praxis haben sich dabei folgende Aspekte erwiesen, die für die Gestaltung der Reihe wesentlich sind:

- Überblick über **Figurenkonstellation**, ggf. **Filmszenen** und **Inhalt**
- **Klausuren** mit **Erwartungshorizont**
- **Arbeitsblätter, Tafelbilder** und **Leitfragen** für den Unterricht
- **Piktogramme** als Hinweise auf **Unterrichts**- und **Arbeitsformen**

Das Prinzip der „**Components**" ermöglicht darüber hinaus den variablen Einsatz der Modelle in unterschiedlich konzipierten Unterrichtsreihen. Dabei stehen Machbarkeit und Praxisnähe stets im Vordergrund.

Das vorliegende Modell bezieht sich auf die DVD *L.A. Crash*. Universum Film 2009

Sprachliche Betreuung: Anne Schülke

www.schoeningh-schulbuch.de
Schöningh Verlag, Jühenplatz 1–3, 33098 Paderborn

Druck 5 4 3 2 / Jahr 2018 17 16 15
Die letzte Zahl bezeichnet das Jahr dieses Druckes.

Umschlaggestaltung: Jennifer Kirchhof
Druck und Bindung: westermann druck GmbH, Braunschweig

ISBN 978-3-14-041168-4

Getting started

"Any real city you walk, you know, you brush past people. People bump into you. In L.A. nobody touches you. [...] We're always behind metal and glass. Think we miss that touch so much, we crash into each other just so we can feel something."

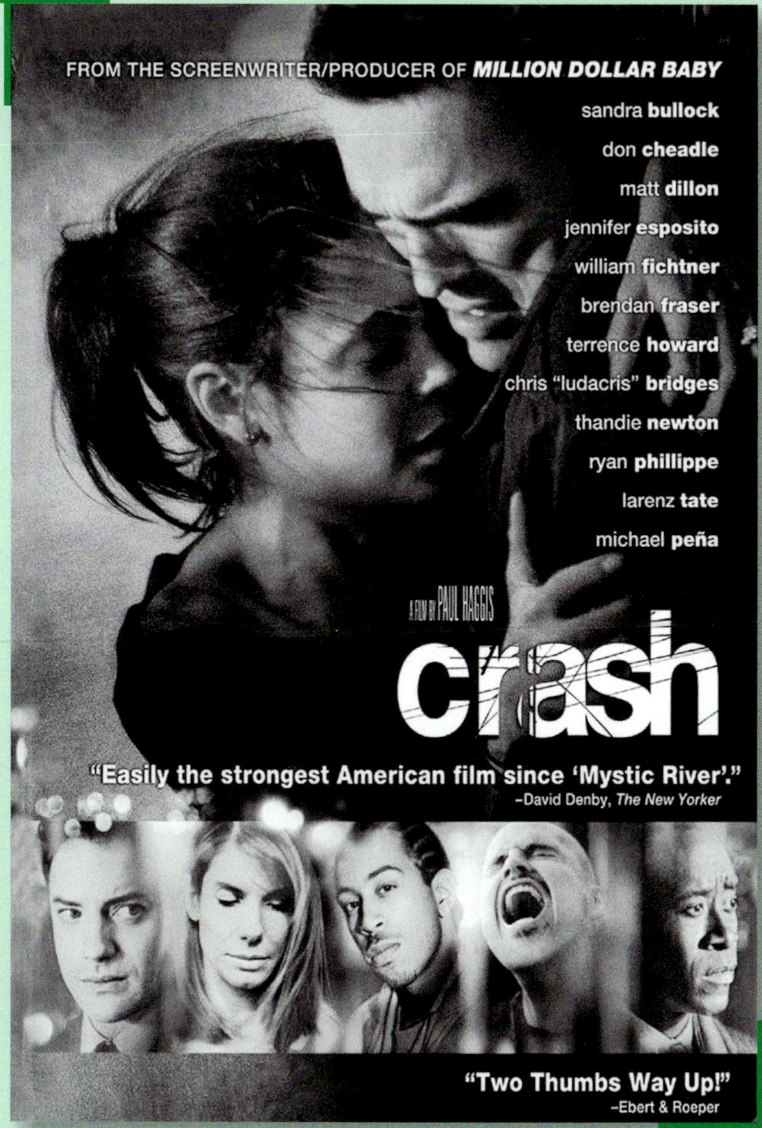

"You can give me the gun or give me the money back, and I'm really hoping for the money."

"[...] if a white person sees two black men walking toward them and turns and walks the other way, she's a racist, right?"

"Who gathered those remarkably different cultures together and taught them all how to park cars on their lawns?"

1. What do title and DVD cover convey about the film in terms of genre and the characters that appear in it? Organize your ideas in a mind map.
2. On the basis of the quotes, speculate about possible topics of the film. Complete the mind map.

L.A. Crash

The film

Synopsis

Set in contemporary multiethnic Los Angeles, Paul Haggis' Oscar-winning film *L.A. Crash* depicts the city's racial and social tensions on an individual level. In a 36-hour period, the lives of strangers usually separated by racial bias and social class coincidentally intersect when the characters physically and emotionally collide in the streets of the megacity. The episodic structure of the drama highlights a continual change in perspective in which victims are exposed as offenders and presumed villains change sides to contradict ethnic stereotyping which is manifested in a fear-based urban society. *L.A. Crash* challenges its audience to question their own ignorance and prejudice to fully understand how destructive modern-day misconceptions of race can be.

Characters and scenarios

<table>
<tr><th>Actors</th><th>Role</th><th>Scenarios</th></tr>
<tr><td>
Sandra Bullock</td><td>Jean Cabot
wife of district attorney Rick Cabot</td><td rowspan="4">Rick manipulates racial politics in L.A. in order to further his career. When he and his wife are carjacked by two African-American youths (Peter and Anthony), Jean's fears of becoming a victim of race-related crime are actualized.
The void in Rick's and Jean's marriage becomes apparent in the argument they have after the theft of their car. There are some allusions to an affair between Rick and his assistant, Karen. His wife feels frustrated and lonely and has to realize that their housekeeper, Maria, is probably the best friend she has.</td></tr>
<tr><td>
Brendan Fraser</td><td>Rick Cabot
local district attorney</td></tr>
<tr><td>
Yomi Perry</td><td>Maria
Latina, housekeeper at the Cabots'</td></tr>
<tr><td>
Nona Gaye</td><td>Karen
Afro-American, Rick's assistant</td></tr>
</table>

 William Fichtner	**Flanagan** head of media relations; works for Rick Cabot	
 Don Cheadle	**Graham Waters** Afro-American, L.A. police detective	Alienated from his drug-addicted mother Louise and his criminal brother Peter, Graham Waters is investigating a shooting in Downtown L.A. while having an affair with his colleague Ria. He is pressurized into forging the results of his investigation by Flanagan. In the end, his mother blames Graham for his younger brother's death.
 Jennifer Esposito	**Ria** Latina, L.A. police detective	
 Beverly Todd	**Louise Waters** Afro-American, Graham's drug-addicted mother	
 Shaun Toub	**Farhad** Persian shopkeeper	Farhad has to face financial ruin when his shop is looted and wrecked. So he puts the blame on the locksmith who had changed the lock, not having been able to convince the other to replace the door and frame. With the gun his daughter has bought for him he seeks revenge and almost kills Daniel's daughter Lara. However, there are only blanks in his gun and the bullet does not harm the little girl. After this incident, Farhad feels released. He tells his daughter Dorri about the "angel" who saved him and hands over the gun to her, saying that he does not need it anymore.
 Bahar Soomekh	**Dorri** Farhad's daughter, a nurse/doctor	
 Michael Peña	**Daniel Ruiz** Latino, locksmith	Daniel Ruiz, a morally upright family man, struggles to find safety for his young family. When he changes the locks at the Cabots' house, he overhears the conversation between Jean and her husband in which Jean makes clear that she does not trust Daniel as she takes him for a gang member. However, Daniel never defends himself against stereotypical thinking or accusations. In order to avoid an escalation, he leaves the shop of the outraged Farhad without being paid. He nearly loses his young daughter Lara when Farhad, who blames the locksmith for the looting of his shop, wants to take revenge on him and shoot him.
 Ashlyn Sánchez	**Lara** Daniel's daughter	

 Loretta Devine	**Shaniqua Johnson** Afro-American; works as an operator for the HMO (Health Maintenance Organization – a low-cost health insurance)	Shaniqua defiantly counters the racist outburst and verbal abuse of officer Ryan who is worried about his father's declining health. John's anguish over an infirm father makes him victimize others by exercising his power. So he makes an unnecessary traffic control in which he humiliates an African-American woman (Christine Thayer) with an invasive body search, while her husband (Cameron) and his partner are forced to stand by powerless. Later, he ironically finds himself rescuing Christine and risking his own life. Dixon is not prepared to compromise his ranking position in the LAPD (which he believes to be a racist organization) when Hansen tells him that Ryan has abused his power.
 Matt Dillon	**John Ryan** LAPD (Los Angeles Police Departement) officer; takes care of his father	
 Ryan Phillippe	**Tom Hansen** LAPD officer, Ryan's colleague	
 Keith David Williams	**Lieutenant Dixon** Afro-American, Ryan's and Hansen's superior	
 Tony Danza	**Fred** producer of Cameron's series	As a white, Fred complains to Cameron that one of their black actors does not speak "black" enough.
 Terrence Howard	**Cameron Thayer** Afro-American, TV producer	The Thayers' marriage is suddenly at stake because the wife accuses her too hesitant husband of not having prevented a racist police officer from molesting her during a traffic control. Their argument causes a personal crisis in Cameron as he feels that there isn't any notion of African-American identity left in his life.
 Thandie Newton	**Christine Thayer** Afro-American/white, Cameron's wife	

<table>
<tr><td>
Christopher Brian Bridges (Ludacris)</td><td>Anthony
Afro-American,
carjacker</td><td rowspan="3">These two youths, coming from an underprivileged background, carjack from whom they believe to be "rich, white folks". To make money, they sell stolen cars to dubious Lucien. Their action has them experience both unexpected awareness and brute force resulting in the death of Peter.</td></tr>
<tr><td>
Larenz Tate</td><td>Peter Waters
Afro-American,
Anthony's friend,
Graham's brother</td></tr>
<tr><td>
Dato Bakhtadze</td><td>Lucien
receiver of stolen cars</td></tr>
</table>

Scene index

1. Detective Graham, Ria	00:00:00	in the car; accident while driving to a scene of crime; Graham investigates
2. Farhad, Dorri	00:05:56	in the gun shop; Farhad wants to buy a gun
3. Peter, Anthony	00:07:46	in the street talking about stereotypes; they carjack Rick's and Jean's vehicle
4. Detective Graham, Ria	00:10:24	on a parking lot; Detective Conklin shot a black colleague called William Lewis; Graham and Ria investigate
5. Jean, Rick, Daniel	00:11:45	at the Cabots'; Daniel changes the locks because the keys were stolen during the carjack; Jean doesn't trust Daniel; she wants the locks to be changed again
6. Rick	00:14:05	at the Cabots'; Rick (district attorney) discusses the election strategy after being carjacked by blacks
7. Officer Ryan, Shaniqua Johnson	00:15:04	in a diner, pay phone next to the door/Shaniqua's office; Ryan calls Shaniqua (an HMO administrator) because of his father's illness
8. O. Ryan, O. Hansen, Cameron, Christine	00:15:55	in the street; police control: the two officers stop Cameron and Christine; Officer Ryan harasses Christine sexually
9. Farhad, Dorri	00:21:58	in Farhad's shop; the door doesn't close
10. Cameron, Christine	00:22:38	in their bedroom; Christine wants to report the incident to the police; Christine criticizes Cameron for not having protected her; she thinks that Cameron obeyed because he didn't want to have the racist attack against him published by the press

11. Daniel, Lara	00:24:26	Daniel arrives at home after a hard day at work; Lara hides under the bed; Daniel makes her believe his story of the invisible cloak that protects her from bullets
12. Peter, Anthony	00:29:22	in Anthony's car; they talk about Hip Hop as "the music of the oppressor"; they run over Choi
13. Officer Hansen, Lt. Dixon	00:32:09	at the police station; Hansen tells Lieutenant Dixon that he does not want to be Ryan's partner anymore
14. Peter, Anthony	00:33:55	Peter and Anthony drop Choi in front of the hospital entrance
15. Daniel, Farhad	00:34:09	in Farhad's shop; Farhad wants Daniel to fix the lock; Daniel advises him to replace the door
16. Peter, Anthony, Lucien	00:35:38	at Lucien's garage; Peter and Anthony want to sell the stolen car to Lucien who refuses because of Choi's blood on the car
17. Detective Graham, Ria	00:36:58	in Graham's bedroom; Graham and Ria are having sex; Graham's mother calls to ask about his brother (Peter); the phone call triggers an argument about identity and racism between Ria and Graham
18. Officer Ryan, his father	00:38:32	in Ryan's flat; Ryan looks after his dad who suffers from an urinary infection
19. Farhad	00:40:12	Farhad enters his shop and finds it ransacked
20. Rick, his assistant Karen	00:40:51	in the Criminal Court Building; while walking down the hall, Rick and Karen talk about the case "Det. Conklin"; Rick asks Karen to send Graham to his office
21. Peter, Anthony	00:41:17	in the street; they talk about how blacks behave in the presence of white people
22. Jean, Maria	00:41:55	in the Cabots' kitchen; Jean criticizes Maria for not having put the dishes into the cupboard
23. Peter, Anthony	00:42:27	in the street; Anthony assumes that buses have big windows just to degrade blacks who take the bus
24. Cameron, Fred	00:43:20	in the film studio; the Executive Producer (Fred) persuades Cameron to take a scene once more because one actor didn't act "black enough"
25. Ryan, Shaniqua	00:44:51	at the HMO administrative offices; Ryan consults Shaniqua again; she refuses to give his father an extra treatment
26. Farhad	00:47:29	in Farhad's shop/company's office; Farhad calls the locksmith's company; he wants to find out the name of their worker who fixed his lock because he suspects him to be behind the break-in
27.–28. Graham, Louise, Ria	00:48:25	in Louise's house; Graham looks in on his mother Louise who is addicted to drugs; she asks Graham if he found his brother; when Graham comes back to the car, Ria tells him that they found something in the Mercedes
29. Cameron, Christine	00:51:25	studio lot; Christine comes to visit Cameron at work during lunch break; she wants to apologize but Cameron does not know how to cope with the situation and leaves her behind

30. Farhad, Dorri	00:53:09	at the shop; the insurance adjuster tells Farhad and Dorri that the insurance will not cover the damage as Farhad did not replace the door although the locksmith told him to do so
31. O. Ryan, O. Hansen	00:54:57	on the parking lot of the police station; Hansen tells Ryan that he has been reassigned; Ryan wishes him good luck but also tells him (as if he wanted to explain his behaviour) that their job makes people change
32. Graham, Ria	00:56:25	police impound garage; a colleague shows Ria and Graham the large amount of money that was hidden in the Mercedes which William Lewis was driving when Detective Conklin shot him
33. Cameron	00:56:47	at the set; Cameron is pensive
34. Farhad	00:57:04	backyard of the shop; Farhad searches the garbage can for the locksmith's bill; thus he finds out that the locksmith's name is Daniel Ruiz
35. Officer Ryan, Christine	00:58:01	in the street; Ryan and his new partner Gomez arrive at a place of accident; Ryan immediately rushes to an overturned car in order to help the driver out of the car – she turns out to be Christine; risking his own life, he saves her from the flames
36. Flanagan, Graham	01:03:52	in the district attorney's conference room; Flanagan (Rick's man in charge of media relations) blackmails Graham to confirm that Detective Conklin's motive to shoot Detective Lewis dead was racism; Flanagan wants him to conceal the fact that the case is more complicated than that and to keep silent about the money they found in the Mercedes; in order to save his brother from being sent to jail for life, he plays along
37. Farhad, Lara, Elizabeth	01:10:07	in front of Daniel's house; Elizabeth leaves the house to meet her daughter who is coming home from school; Farhad observes the scene from his car
38. Anthony, Peter, Cameron, Tom	01:10:35	Anthony and Peter want to carjack Cameron's car but Cameron defends himself and his car; when the police approach, Peter runs away but Cameron and Anthony get into the car and try to escape; while Cameron gets out and provokes one of the policemen, Anthony stays in the car; Officer Hansen recognizes Cameron and lets him go with a warning; before Cameron drops Anthony off he gives him back the gun telling him that he embarrassed him
39. Farhad, Lara, Daniel, Elizabeth	01:17:23	when Daniel comes home, Farhad gets out of his car and threatens Daniel with his gun; Lara, who observes this from inside the house, runs towards her father, falling into his arms when Farhad pulls the trigger; surprisingly nothing happens to Lara nor to Daniel and they go back into the house; Farhad remains outside astonished and confused
40. Graham	01:20:12	Graham fills his mother's fridge with groceries he bought; Louise is sleeping on the sofa

41. Jean	01:20:48	at the Cabots'; Jean is on the phone talking to her friend Carol and telling her that she's in a depressed mood; Carol has to interrupt the phone call as she's going to have a massage; after the phone call Jean falls down the stairs
42. Officer Ryan	01:22:22	Ryan in his car; pensive
43. Peter, Officer Hansen	01:23:23	Peter hitch-hikes; Hansen gives him a lift; when Peter reaches into his pocket to show why he is laughing, Hansen shoots him dead thinking that he wants to pull out his gun
44. Graham	01:27:16	at the scene of the crime (see scene 1); Graham finds his brother's dead body
45. Anthony	01:28:09	Anthony in the bus; he gets off when he discovers Choi's ("the Chinaman's") van in the street
46. Kim Lee, Choi	01:29:04	at the hospital; Kim Lee finds her husband; he tells her to immediately cash the check he has in his shirt
47. Lucien, Anthony	01:30:06	at Lucien's garage; Anthony wants to sell the Chinaman's van to Lucien; when they discover illegal aliens (Asians) in the back of the van, Lucien offers Anthony 500 dollars for each and explains that he wants to sell them
48. Louise, Graham, Ria, Dorri	01:30:57	at the hospital; Louise cries as she has just seen her younger son's dead body; Graham cannot calm her down; Louise reproaches Graham for not having the time to find his brother; Graham leaves; Dorri comes out of one of the rooms (she is a nurse or doctor) to call home
49. Dorri, Farhad	01:33:17	at the shop; Farhad tells his daughter what happened; he thinks that Lara is the angel who saved him and hands Dorri the gun; she takes the gun and the bullets (blanks) with her
50. Rick and Jean	01:35:24	at the Cabots'/in the Criminal Court Building; Jean calls Rick to tell him that she fell down the stairs and that her friend Carol let her down; Rick promises to come home; Jean hugs her housekeeper Maria and tells her that she is her best friend
51. Officer Hansen	01:37:13	Officer Hansen burns his car to destroy all evidence of his deed
52. – 54. Officer Ryan, Rick, Daniel	01:37:44	• at Officer Ryan's house; Ryan comforts his father • Rick at home looking out of the window • at Daniel's home; Lara sleeps close to her mum in her parents' bed; Daniel is awake, looking out of the window
55. Cameron, Christine	01:38:32	Cameron sees children playing around the burning car; he calls Christine to tell her that he loves her; she is at home and starts crying saying that she loves him too
56. Graham	01:40:24	at the scene of the crime; Graham discovers Peter's talisman: a statuette of Saint Christopher
57. Anthony	01:41:21	in a city street; Anthony releases the illegal aliens
58. Shaniqua	01:43:03	a car collides with Shaniqua's car; she tells the Hispanic occupants to speak "American"

Das Unterrichtsmodell

Vorüberlegungen zum Einsatz des Films im Unterricht

Der Film *L.A. Crash* ist Teil des Abitur-Schwerpunktthemas *Challenges and Choices in an Insecure World* an allgemeinbildenden Gymnasien in Baden-Württemberg. Die Themenvielfalt, die der Film bietet, macht ihn jedoch für die gymnasiale Kursstufe in allen Bundesländern attraktiv. Es bietet sich an, den Film bei soziokulturellen Themenschwerpunkten wie *living in a multiethnic immigrant society, living in a big city, racism* oder *the American Dream* in den Unterricht zu integrieren. Nicht zuletzt eignet sich *L.A. Crash* aufgrund seiner Episodenstruktur auch hervorragend zur genaueren filmanalytischen Betrachtung.

So wie die Protagonisten im Film immer wieder ihre Haltung und Vorurteile überdenken müssen, ist auch der Zuschauer stets gefordert, seine eigenen Moralvorstellungen und Sichtweisen zu relativieren und zu revidieren. Durch die multiperspektivische Struktur liefert der Film keine allgemeingültige Schlussfolgerung, sondern überlässt es dem Zuschauer, über richtig oder falsch, sympathisch oder unsympathisch zu urteilen. Mit der Behandlung des Films im Unterricht werden also nicht nur sprachliche, filmanalytische und interpretatorische Fertigkeiten der Schüler gefördert, sondern auch ihre Empathie- und Selbstreflexionsfähigkeit sowie ihre interkulturelle Kompetenz in besonderem Maße trainiert.

Der Film kam in den USA unter dem Namen *Crash* in die Kinos, während für den deutschsprachigen Raum der Titel *L.A. Crash* gewählt wurde. Um das urbane Setting zu verdeutlichen, wird auch im vorliegenden Unterrichtsmodell die Bezeichnung *L.A. Crash* verwendet. Alle Zeitangaben im *Scene index* und auf den Arbeitsblättern beziehen sich auf die in Deutschland problemlos zu erhaltende DVD *L.A. Crash* der Universum Film, 2009. Die Zeitangaben wurden durch das Abspielen mit dem *Windows Media Player* ermittelt. Die DVD enthält den Film in der englischen Originalversion, die deutsche Synchronfassung, englische und deutsche Untertitel sowie *Special Features* (Filmtrailer, Interviews, Musikvideo).

Dieses Modell ist für den Einsatz in der Kursstufe/gymnasialen Oberstufe ausgerichtet, weshalb Grundkenntnisse in der Filmanalyse und die entsprechenden sprachlichen Mittel vorausgesetzt werden. Das *fact sheet* (***Copy 6***, S. 61) beinhaltet die wichtigsten Termini und kann den Schülern bei Bedarf ausgeteilt werden.

Konzeption des Unterrichtsmodells

Die strukturelle und inhaltliche Komplexität des Episodenfilms *L.A. Crash* macht eine Analyse einzelner Handlungsstränge unumgänglich. Damit die Schüler die Zusammenhänge der vielschichtigen Handlung herstellen können, erscheint eine möglichst frühe Präsentation des gesamten Films ratsam. In einem zweiten Schritt wird durch das nochmalige, genauere Schauen einzelner Sequenzen und den Vergleich von ausgewählten Szenen eine zielgerichtete Betrachtung verschiedener thematischer Aspekte möglich.

Das vorliegende Unterrichtsmodell ist so konzipiert, dass der Film entweder im Unterricht abschnittsweise mit der Klasse angeschaut werden kann *(Component 1)* oder nach einem gemeinsamen Einstieg gleich in Gänze präsentiert wird. Dies ist somit der schnellere Weg zu einer vertieften thematischen Analyse *(Components 2* und *3)*, wie er etwa mit leistungsstärkeren Klassen eingeschlagen werden kann.

Component 1 wird filmbegleitend eingesetzt, wobei das Hör-/Sehverstehen durch geschlossene und offenere Aufgabenformate gezielt geschult wird. Bereits die ersten Aufeinandertreffen der Protagonisten machen deutlich, dass das Zusammenleben von Vorurteilen, rassistischen Übergriffen und Kriminalität geprägt ist, was sich durch den ganzen Film hindurch zieht. Gebildete Hypothesen müssen dabei immer wieder revidiert und adaptiert werden.

Der thematische Schwerpunkt von ***Component 2*** liegt auf der Analyse der Protagonisten und deren Entwicklung im Verlauf des Films sowie auf deren Zuschauerwirkung. Wie die Charaktere mit persönlichen Herausforderungen, die sich durch Interaktionen im sozialen und familiären Umfeld ergeben, zurechtkommen und welche Entscheidungen sie treffen, wird durch die Analyse einzelner exemplarischer Szenen genauer betrachtet. Vor allem bei den Wiederbegegnungen kommen die unterschiedlichen Facetten der Figuren zum Vorschein. Die familiären Hintergründe sind in diesem Zusammenhang aufschlussreich. Durch den Vergleich der im Film dargestellten urbanen Familienmodelle werden Implikationen aufgegriffen und semantische Leerstellen auf kreative Weise gefüllt.

Während sich *Component 2* mit Herausforderungen und Problemen auf der Mikroebene beschäftigt, steht in ***Component 3*** die Analyse makrostruktureller Beziehungen im Vordergrund. Dabei wird das analytische Spektrum zunehmend erweitert. Es wird die Frage betrachtet, warum die Begegnungen der Charaktere mit unterschiedlichen soziokulturellen Hintergründen stets von Aggression, Ablehnung und Intoleranz gekennzeichnet sind. Dazu wird das Konzept *Bigotry* eingeführt und ausgewählte Szenen werden dahin gehend genauer analysiert. Durch Impulse zu landeskundlichem Hintergrundwissen können die Schüler schließlich die Filmszenen in einen globaleren Zusammenhang einordnen und deren Realitätsbezug bewerten.

In ***Component 4*** laufen alle Fäden zusammen: Die Schüler entwerfen ein Konzept für einen Trailer zum Film und greifen so thematisch wichtige Aspekte wieder auf. Darüber hinaus setzen sie ihre filmanalytischen Kenntnisse aktiv und produktiv ein.

Weiterführende Materialien

- **Burwitz-Melzer, Eva (2009)**: „Film Puzzles: Episodenfilme im Fremdsprachenunterricht", in: Leitzke-Ungerer, Eva (Hrsg.): *Film im Fremdsprachenunterricht – Literarische Stoffe, interkulturelle Ziele, mediale Wirkung.* Stuttgart: ibidem-Verlag, S. 277–294.
  → methodische Hinweise zur Arbeit mit Episodenfilmen im Fremdsprachenunterricht am Beispiel des Films *L.A. Crash*

- **Farris, Christine (2007)**: "Crash Course: Race, Class, and Context", in: *College English,* 69 (4), S. 354–359. Herunterladbar unter: http://web4.uwindsor.ca/users /w/winter/Film.nsf/0/f68fa7d7b35831b98525785b00639bb7/$FILE/Crash%20Course%20Race,%20Class,%20and%20Context.pdf
  → Essay, welcher zentrale Themen von *L.A. Crash* kritisch darstellt

- **Goyette, Tori (2011)**: "White Power: An Analysis of Racial Tensions in *Crash*", herunterladbar unter: http://ejournals.bc.edu/ojs/index.php/freshink/article/view/ 1207/1580
  → filmkritischer Essay; Originalversion des Textes von Klausur 1

- **Hansalek, Tanja/Hansalek, Erik (2011):** „Hey, you gotta see this – Analyse der Werbefunktion von Trailern", in: *Der Fremdsprachliche Unterricht Englisch,* 112/113, S. 51–55.
  → Methoden zur Arbeit mit Trailern im Fremdsprachenunterricht; Kriterien von Filmtrailern

- **Henseler, Roswitha (2011):** „Die Verbindung von Bild und Ton: Förderung von ‚Hör-Seh-Verstehen' als Teil von Filmverstehen im Englischunterricht", in: *Der Fremdsprachliche Unterricht Englisch,* 112/113, S. 2–12.
  → Artikel zur Kompetenz Hör-/Sehverstehen als Voraussetzung für die Analyse der filmischen Inhalte und Darstellungsverfahren; rezeptive und produktive Filmarbeit

- **Henseler, Roswitha (2011):** „Coming attractions – Unterstützungsangebote für die Analyse von Filmtrailern", in: *Der Fremdsprachliche Unterricht Englisch,* 112/113, S. 46–50.
  → didaktische und methodische Anregungen zur Arbeit mit Filmtrailern

- **Stempleski, Susan/Tomalin, Barry (2001):** *Film.* Oxford: Oxford University Press.
  → sehr umfangreiche, praxisnahe Unterrichtsideen zur Arbeit mit Filmen

- **Szeto, Andy (2006):** *Crash curriculum guide,* herunterladbar unter: http://szetohistory.tripod.com/CrashUnits.pdf
  → Unterrichtsentwurf eines Highschool-Lehrers mit vielen weiterführenden themenorientierten Anregungen

- Software-CD *Close-Up: L.A. Crash* (2013), Schöningh-Verlag.
  → ermöglicht eine interaktive Filmanalyse in den Bereichen *literary aspects, dramatic aspects* und *cinematic aspects*

- http://www.awesomefilm.com/script/Crash.pdf
  → Drehbuch zum Film *L.A. Crash* (Anmerkung: Reihenfolge der Szenen im Drehbuch stimmt teilweise nicht mit Film überein)

- http://www.filmeducation.org/pdf/film/Crash.pdf
  → Hintergrundinformationen zu Themen, Figuren und Plot in *L.A. Crash*

- http://mediaandenglishatlakes.blogspot.de/2007_09_01_archive.html
  → Blog zum Film *L.A. Crash,* u.a. englische Titel der Kapitel mit Zusammenfassung der Szeneninhalte, *film editing* (Episodenstruktur), Beschreibung der einzelnen Handlungsstränge, *set design (props), setting* L.A.

- http://www.lacrash-filmschool.de/
  → Online-Selbstlernmodul für Schülerinnen und Schüler der Sekundarstufe II, welches Filmbildung und interkulturelles Lernen miteinander verknüpft; Projektleitung: Englisches Seminar Leibniz Universität Hannover

- http://www.film-zeit.de/Film/15851/LA-CRASH/Kritik/
  → Linksammlung zu Filmkritiken von *L.A. Crash* in deutscher Sprache

- http://www.tolerance.org/
  → Unterrichtsmaterialien zum Thema *tolerance,* u. a. *bigotry*

- http://www.youtube.com/watch?v=VDJZem3mq2M
  → Trailer zum Film *Crossing over,* welcher ähnliche Thematiken aufgreift wie *L.A. Crash*

- http://lehrerfortbildunq-bw.de/werkstatt/video/unterricht/baum/ideenpool/
  → Ideenpool zur Filmarbeit mit Schülerinnen und Schülern (Landesakademie für Fortbildung und Personalentwicklung an Schulen, Baden-Württemberg)

(Letzter Zugriff auf alle Internetquellen: Mai 2013)

Klausur und Kommunikationsprüfung

Die folgenden zwei Klausurvorschläge können zur Leistungsüberprüfung nach der Unterrichtseinheit eingesetzt werden. Beide orientieren sich an den schriftlichen Aufgabenformaten des Abiturs in Baden-Württemberg.

Klausur 1 besteht aus drei Teilen, für deren Bearbeitung den Schülern zwei bis drei Schulstunden zur Verfügung gestellt werden sollten. Er ist eher für einen Englischkurs mit gutem Leistungsniveau oder zur Vorbereitung auf das schriftliche Abitur ausgelegt. Text 1 ist ein Essay einer amerikanischen Studentin, die der Rechtfertigung rassistischen Verhaltens im Film *L.A. Crash* kritisch gegenübersteht. Das Leseverstehen *(Comprehension)* wird überprüft, indem die Schüler wesentliche Aussagen zu diesem Text auf ihre Richtigkeit hin untersuchen. Für den Analyseteil *(Analysis)* wird mit Text 2 ein weiterer Impuls geliefert. Es handelt sich um eine deutsche Filmkritik, die ebenfalls – wenn auch mit anderer Argumentation als die Studentin – Schwächen des Films *L.A. Crash* herausarbeitet. Der Autor des Textes bemängelt, dass am Ende alles geordnet und jede Handlung erklärbar erscheint, weshalb es dem Film nicht gelingen kann, das Bild einer komplexen multiethnischen, urbanen Gesellschaft in realistischer beziehungsweise naturalistischer Art nachzuzeichnen. Die Schüler fassen die Hauptaussagen des deutschen Textes knapp auf Englisch zusammen *(Mediation)* und vergleichen ihn mit dem Text der Studentin. Im dritten Teil *(Composition)* haben die Schüler die Wahl: Sie können sich für eine kreative Schreibaufgabe entscheiden, bei der sie sich in Christine Thayer hineinversetzen und aus ihrer Perspektive den Polizisten John Ryan und ihren Ehemann Cameron beurteilen. Alternativ können die Schüler in der analytischen Schreibaufgabe herausarbeiten, ob beziehungsweise inwieweit sich *L.A. Crash* ausschließlich auf die amerikanische Gesellschaft bezieht. Es werden also Aspekte und Methoden aus den behandelten Themen verschiedener *Components* aufgegriffen *(racism, how characters develop, diary entries, urban life)*, gleichzeitig verlangen die Aufgaben aber auch Transferleistungen der Schüler.

Die **Kommunikationsprüfung 2** dient neben der Überprüfung der Unterrichtsinhalte v. a. der Feststellung kommunikativer Kompetenzen. Angelehnt an das Format der Kommunikationsprüfung in Baden-Württemberg, welche dort ab 2014 Bestandteil der Abiturprüfung ist, stellen die Schüler in einer paarweise durchgeführten Prüfung ihre Filmkenntnisse und zugleich die Rede- und Diskussionsfähigkeit unter Beweis.
Die Prüfung untergliedert sich in eine monologische und eine dialogische Phase. Zur Vorbereitung auf die Prüfung erhalten die beiden Schüler je unterschiedliche Versionen des ersten Teils von Klausur 2 *(1. Sequenz: Monologisches Sprechen)* sowie ein einsprachiges Wörterbuch. Ausgehend von zwei *Screenshots* zu jeweils einer Filmfigur (Officer John Ryan und Inspector Graham Waters) bereiten sie einen Kurzvortrag vor, bei dem das Filmwissen im Vordergrund steht. Diese Prüfungsphase zielt auf die Charakterisierung der ausgewählten Figuren ab, wobei deren Entwicklungen im Verlauf des Films sowie die Begegnungen mit anderen Figuren und die sich daraus ergebenden Herausforderungen des Zusammenlebens im urbanen Raum im Vordergrund stehen (vgl. *Components 1 + 2).*
Die zweite Prüfungsphase kann recht offen gestaltet werden. Prinzipiell ist jegliche Art von Erörterung oder Diskussion in Anlehnung an den Film möglich. Sollte sich in der monologischen Prüfungsphase bereits ein Thema herauskristallisiert haben, kann dieses von den Schülern sogleich aufgegriffen werden. Naheliegend ist im ersten Schritt ein Vergleich der beiden Charaktere bezüglich ihrer Stellung in der Gesellschaft. Damit das Gespräch nicht

abflacht oder um weiterführende Aspekte einzubringen, kann unter anderem das abgedruckte Zitat des Regisseurs Paul Haggis als Impuls vorgelegt werden. Es spricht das Thema *living together in a multicultural society/bigotry* an. Darüber hinaus betont es den Perspektivwechsel, den der Film dem Zuschauer ermöglicht. Dieses Hineinversetzen in die Charaktere rückt das Individuum in den Vordergrund, wobei die soziokulturellen Differenzen unbedeutend sind.
Die Formulierung „My aim with this film is …" lässt eine Bewertung der Aussage bezüglich der gelungenen beziehungsweise nicht gelungenen Umsetzung zu und bietet damit eine Diskussionsgrundlage. Schließlich kann das Thema *urban challenges* vertieft werden, indem ausgehend von den Herausforderungen, mit denen sich die beschriebenen Charaktere konfrontiert sehen, weitere Beispiele aus dem Film angeführt werden. Diskussionswürdig sind sicherlich manche *choices,* die die Charaktere als Reaktionen auf die *challenges* wählen.
Die folgenden Zeitangaben sind Richtwerte, welche dem Leistungsstand der Schüler angepasst werden können.

Vorbereitungszeit:	15 Minuten (einsprachiges Wörterbuch)
Prüfungszeit:	*Phase 1 (monologisches Sprechen)*: pro Schüler ca. 5 Minuten
	Phase 2 (dialogisches Sprechen): insgesamt ca. 10 Minuten

Als Bewertungsgrundlage für die sprachlichen Kompetenzen kann die Niveaueinteilung des Gemeinsamen Europäischen Referenzrahmens dienen.

1 Tori Goyette: White Power: An Analysis of Racial Tensions in *Crash*

In 2004 Paul Haggis directed the Oscar-winning film *Crash,* a drama fundamentally about race and its effects on various people in Los Angeles. The acclaimed movie earned rave reviews from average viewers, as it asked hard questions about racism on an individual level and showed some harsh realities that are usually avoided on the big screen. The movie promotes racial awareness, but like any conversation about race, it demands close inspection. [...]

We do not learn very much about each character in *Crash,* but we know enough to figure out how Haggis wants us to understand them. We see a variety of African American men and women, several Hispanic characters, a Persian family, and several Asians. A scene will switch to another only because the initial characters' story line is intersecting with that of the next. [...]

Critics receive the film very differently. Victor Villanueva, in *College English,* wrote about the limitations in Haggis' attempts to present racism: Most of the characters are provided with life circumstances to help us see where they are coming from. The circumstances include Officer Ryan's sick father, Jean Cabot's depression, and the shopkeeper's struggle with being a new immigrant. Each serves as an excuse for the characters' racism (or at least a way to lessen its severity). [...] Villanueva argues that illness, depression, fear, and poverty do [not] make racism excusable. These are to him insufficient attempts to find reasons for immoral behavior. The film's effort to rationalize intolerance leaves its potential for a powerful message about racism feeling incomplete and shortchanged. *Crash* presents many races and their intersections, but the white characters appear to be less complex, and ultimately more forgivable, than the other races. I have chosen to analyze Haggis' objectives with the portrayal of white characters.

The first white characters we meet are Jean and Rick Cabot, an L.A. District Attorney and his wife, played by Brendan Fraser and Sandra Bullock. These are beautiful, confident, well-off characters whose social status is evident at first sight. Jean grabs her husband's arm upon seeing two young black men in the street and Anthony, played by Ludacris, notes she is a typical racist white woman for expressing her fear in such a safe place. Anthony goes on to steal her car. In a sense, Haggis demonstrates Jean's racism by having her clutch her husband for security, but goes on to right her decision when the black men actualize her fears. We do not leave the scene feeling her actions were reprehensible. [...] Haggis allows the worst to happen. No breaking down of stereotypes takes place, in fact quite the opposite. [...]

Ultimately the movie doesn't leave us with a bad feeling about Jean while she progresses as a stereotypical white, privileged woman who doesn't work. Towards the end, Jean complains tirelessly about all the different domestic helpers (who we are supposed to assume are not white) and why they aren't meeting her demands. She speaks in a way that both suggests and affirms her white privilege. In this scene she realizes it is not the people and the world around her, but in fact she is simply an unhappy woman. She begins to cry, and we see her change. Next she is giving her Hispanic housekeeper a hug and calling the woman her best friend. The scene takes this white character and paints her in a more positive light. I personally do not believe personal troubles to be an excuse for racism, and Haggis may not either, but all the same he presents this chiastic structure with white characters: they act with racist behavior, and then ultimately undo it after a certain breaking point (in Jean's case, falling down the stairs). [...]

Haggis does not unpack the characters in a way that gives evidence of their individual transformations; we merely see them going through tough times and [...] respond according to empathy we feel towards them based on experiences in our own lives. [...]

Viewers might take comfort in the notion that everyone is a little bit racist. *Crash* is not filled with accusations; it is a film of dismissals. The message seems to be that everyone has racism in them, but everyone can still be a good person. [...]

acclaimed (*adj.*) praised enthusiastically

rave review an article in a newspaper or magazine that is very enthusiastic about a particular film

reprehensible (*adj.*) morally wrong, deserving criticism

chiastic (*adj.*) here: repeated in reverse order

dismissal (*n.*) the failure to consider something as important

This is not a movie about systematic racism in a white-dominant culture, and it certainly could be. It may be that Haggis foresaw the popularity of the film and thought depicting white people as villains might hurt his favorable reviews. [...] In a film meant to leave a mark and ignite relevant and important conversations about race, white people are let off the hook in *Crash,* as it happens in real life. *(776 words)*

In: *Fresh Ink Essays From Boston College's First-Year Writing Seminar,* Vol 13, No 3 (2011).
http://napoleon.bc.edu/ojs/index.php/freshink/article/view/1207/1580 [04.07.2013]
(Text abridged and slightly modified. For reasons of a better legibility the works cited are not indicated in the text and thus not enlisted here. However, they are accessible under the given link.)

2 Daniel Haas: Kinodrama *L.A. Crash*: Gottes Crashtest-Dummys

[...] „L.A. Crash", das Regiedebüt des Drehbuchautors Paul Haggis, will [...] ein Film der urbanen Kollisionen sein, ein Szenario der Zusammenstöße. [...] Gleich zu Beginn erklärt der schwarze Polizist (Don Cheadle) seiner Kollegin, einer Latina (Jennifer Esposito), dass die Menschen, eingesperrt in ihren Autos, am Leben und an sich selbst vorbeidriften. Nur ein Zusammenstoß könne sie aus diesem Dilemma befreien. Die Kollision als Katastrophe und Katharsis, das ist nicht besonders subtil, und tatsächlich ist „L.A. Crash" in seiner Dramaturgie so plakativ wie ein Thesenpapier.

Zur Debatte stehen die multiethnische Gesellschaft und die sie beherrschenden Spannungen von Rasse, Klasse und Geschlecht. Dafür werden die Einzelschicksale episodisch so choreografiert, dass jeder ausgiebig zu Wort kommt: der Staatsanwalt (Brendan Fraser), der einen Mord in den eigenen Reihen vertuscht; der Ermittler (Cheadle), dessen Mutter der Drogensucht verfällt; der junge Polizist (Ryan Phillippe), der seinen von Rassenhass zerfressenen Partner (Matt Dillon) verabscheut und am Ende selbst rassistisch handelt.

Auf den ersten Blick scheint der Film ein komplexes Bild gesellschaftlicher Schuldzusammenhänge zu vermitteln, die der Einzelne nicht überschauen kann [...]. Doch der extreme Realismus der Darstellung, die inszenatorische Härte sind nur ein Bluff: „L.A. Crash" will nicht die neue Unübersichtlichkeit der Schmelztiegelgesellschaft und deren Gefährdungen aufzeigen, sondern eine Utopie bebildern. Die zeigt sich weniger auf der Inhaltsebene der einzelnen Episoden, die exzellent gespielt und in ihrem Naturalismus teilweise erschütternd sind, als in der Struktur des Films.

In Haggis' Welt waltet eine Schicksalssymmetrie, die schließlich allen den richtigen Platz zuweist. [...] Überwölbt von einem sakral wabernden Soundtrack, macht diese Erzählung deutlich: Mögen Menschen auch in sinnloser Gewalt kollidieren, mögen ihre Handlungen von Gier und Rachsucht bestimmt sein – [eine] übergeordnete Instanz lenkt alles in einen sinnvollen Zusammenhang.

Deshalb ist „L.A. Crash" letztlich kein naturalistisches, sondern ein metaphorisches Projekt. Es setzt Figuren als Statthalter für die große amerikanische Hoffnung ein, am Ende doch das große soziale Experiment der Neuzeit zu sein, in der ein gerechtes Leben über die Grenzen von Hautfarbe und Herkunft möglich ist. [...] *(332 words)*

SPIEGEL ONLINE, Daniel Haas, 04. August 2005

Assignments

1. Comprehension (10 VP)

Read text 1.
Decide whether the following statements are true or false. In your own words, give reasons for your decisions and indicate the lines where you found the relevant information.

1. Both cinema-goers and critics praised *L.A. Crash* enthusiastically.

___

___

___

___

2. According to a critic, individual problems of the characters are given as justifications of racial prejudice and discrimination.

___

___

___

___

3. The author of the text implies that the director's interpretation of Jean Cabot reinforces existing clichés.

___

___

___

___

4. The author is of the opinion that Haggis gives a detailed description of the characters' development and the audience understands their feelings due to similar happenings in their own lives.

___

___

___

___

5. According to the author, Haggis depicts white people as villains to trigger a discussion about racism.

2. Analysis (10 VP)

Sum up the main aspects of the article from the German online magazine *Spiegel Online*, focusing on the weaker points the author sees in *L.A. Crash*. Compare his assessments of the film to Tori Goyette's in text 1.

3. Composition (10 VP)

Choose one of the two tasks.

a) After her accident Christine is overwhelmed by the incidents of the last hours. She needs to sort herself out. This is why she entrusts her thoughts to her diary. Write Christine's diary entry expressing her feelings about the accident, about Officer Ryan and about her husband.

OR

b) *L.A. Crash* is a film which offers only insight into the American society. Discuss this view.

Erwartungshorizont zu Klausur 1

Zu 1 (Comprehension)

1. This statement is false. Although the film received good reviews by ordinary viewers, it couldn't win some critics' approval. (ll. 2–4, 12–13)

2. This statement is true. Both the critic Victor Villanueva and the author herself think that personal problems are no reasons to pardon racist behaviour. (ll. 17–19)

3. This statement is true. In the author's view, Haggis justifies Jean's behaviour by making come true what she is afraid of. (l. 32)

4. This statement is false. According to the author of the text, Haggis' way of presentation does not explain character development but only depicts the characters in different situations, making the audience understand them because of similar experiences. (ll. 47–49)

5. This statement is false. Tori Goyette argues that, in the end, *L.A. Crash* is not a film about racism as all the white characters are provided with an excuse for their reprehensible behaviour. Goyette accuses Haggis of having chosen to do so in order to receive positive reviews. (ll. 50–55)

Zu 2 (Analysis)

Lösungsvorschlag:

In his review Daniel Haas argues that, at first sight, the film *L.A. Crash* succeeds in drawing a picture of a complex, chaotic, urban society where coincidence determines whose lives intersect with each other. It shows a society full of tensions between races, social classes and genders; a society where people, according to the situation, take different roles: they are rescuers, pursuers and murderers. If in one scene the characters are shown as villains, in another scene they turn out to have a good side as well and vice versa. For Haas it seems as if everything, racism as well as violence, are predestined so that in the end everybody can find his place in the social structure. This is why he thinks that *L.A. Crash* does not come up to the raised expectations as it does not succeed in depicting the real complexity of a melting pot society and its dangers. Thus, Haas concludes, *L.A. Crash* is rather a metaphor for the American hope that a life beyond the boundaries of skin colour and origin is possible, which, the author thinks, is naïve.

Whereas Daniel Haas thinks that, due to its structure, *L.A. Crash* does not manage to show society in a realistic, naturalistic way, Tori Goyette sees its weaknesses in the way the characters are portrayed. She accuses director Paul Haggis of excusing his characters' racist behaviour with personal trials and tribulations to make the (white) audience forgive them. Thus racism is depicted as something normal and justifiable; the problem is played down.

Zu 3 (Composition)

a) individuelle Lösungen

b) mögliche Antworten:

L.A. Crash offers only insight into the American society:	The film also depicts universal topics:
• failure of institutions: American healthcare system (compare with Ryan's problem) • specific situation of blacks in the USA • today: emancipation (Shaniqua, the Thayers, Graham) and discrimination • Los Angeles presented as a big city which, as an urban jungle, cannot be compared to German cities because of its size, ethnic diversity, institutions, etc. • ethnic diversity as a mirror of American society • human trafficking as a major American problem (compare to the Asians Anthony finds in the van)	• father-son relationship • deficient family relationships • problems of well-to-do people like the Cabots • crime as a topic of other big cities, in Europe for example • gun control is a problem in Germany as well (compare rampages in Winnenden, Erfurt or other schools)

Kommunikationsprüfung

Student A

1. Sequenz: Monologisches Sprechen

Produce an uninterrupted 5-minute discourse based on the two screenshots below. Describe the character. Point out the challenges John Ryan faces in the film and how they influence him and the people he 'crashes' into.

1

2

Student B

1. Sequenz: Monologisches Sprechen

Produce an uninterrupted 5-minute discourse based on the two screenshots below. Describe the character. Point out the challenges Graham Waters faces in the film and how they influence him and the people he 'crashes' into.

1

2

2. Sequenz: Dialogisches Sprechen

Zusätzliche Impulse, die bei Bedarf von der Lehrkraft gegeben werden können:

Impuls 1

They may be black and white, but actually they are the same. Discuss!

Impuls 2

It's the challenges of urban life that shape our identity. Discuss!

Impuls 3

"My aim with this film is to explore how intolerance is a collective problem. I did not set out to offend or ignite controversy, but to look at many different people, each with his or her unique perspective. Film enables us to walk, however briefly, in the shoes of strangers. In that sense, I hope that Crash succeeds not so much in pointing out differences, but in recognizing our shared humanity."
(Paul Haggis, director of *Crash*)
http://www.reviewexpress.com/review.php?rv=124 [05.07.2013]

In how far did Paul Haggis achieve his aim?

Impuls 4

"A certain level of indifference makes possible personal freedom and a tolerant multicultural city."
(Bart van Leeuwen, Radboud University Nijmegen, Netherlands)

Discuss.

Erwartungshorizont zur Kommunikationsprüfung 2

Zu 1: Sequenz (Monologisches Sprechen)

Student A

- Officer John Ryan:
  - police officer
  - in his forties
  - cares for his father who suffers from a urinary infection
  - racist tendencies

- Screenshot no. 1:
  - Ryan is at Shaniqua's office at the HMO.
  - He apologizes for insulting her on the phone the day before and tells her his father's life story. Nevertheless, Ryan cannot convince Shaniqua to approve of a better treatment for his father.
  - challenges he faces: family (caring son); failure of institutions (HMO refuses a proper treatment for his father)

- Screenshot no. 2:
  - Ryan rescues a woman out of her damaged car. When he climbs into the overturned car, he realizes that it is Christine, the woman he harassed sexually the night before.
  - "From zero to hero?"
  - Challenges he faces: Ryan is confronted with his misbehaviour by coincidentally meeting again the woman he sexually harassed the day before

Student B

- Detective Graham Waters:
  - detective inspector
  - African-American
  - in his thirties
  - family: mother (addicted to drugs), his brother Peter (criminal), Ria (his girlfriend?)

- Screenshot no. 1:
  - Graham and his mother are in the hospital to see Peter's dead body (Peter was shot by Hansen because of a chain of mishaps).
  - When Louise sees Peter, she collapses and blames Graham for not being interested in their family.
  - challenges he faces: dysfunctional family

- Screenshot no. 2:
  - Graham at the district attorney's office
  - Flanagan, member of the district attorney's staff, blackmails Graham. Context: A black colleague was shot by a white colleague, Detective Conklin. To save the votes of the black electorate in the next election, the district attorney Rick Cabot wants Conklin to be punished appropriately. As the investigations are rather complicated, Graham first refuses to convict Conklin. When Flanagan shows him the outstanding warrant against his criminal brother Peter and promises to make it disappear if Graham approves, he agrees.
  - challenges he faces: solidarity with his brother vs. solidarity with his colleague; maintaining his duties as an inspector

Zu 2: Sequenz (Dialogisches Sprechen)

Impuls 1 They may be black and white, but actually they are the same. Discuss!

Similarities
- both work for the state (police officer/detective inspector)
- both are members of the middle class (but: black vs. white, cf. differences)
- both have to care for their parents with devotion, both parents are single
- both struggle with the challenges of urban life (multicultural society, bigotry, social injustice, failure of institutions, corruption, (dys-)functional families …)
- both try to overcome personal and global challenges to lead a meaningful life
- both are still in the process of self-discovery ("You think you know who you are? You have no idea.")

Differences
- Graham is African-American, John is white
- racism: Graham is a victim (blackmailed by his superior); Ryan is a victimizer (discriminates against Shaniqua; harasses Christine at the police control)
- Graham stays in the position of the suppressed/unloved son, Ryan changes drastically in the course of the film (first harasses Christine, then rescues her) → his impression on the audience changes (likeable/unlikeable)
- Graham rather avoids conflicts, John mostly reacts aggressively

Impuls 2 It's the challenges of urban life that shape our identity. Discuss!

Challenges of urban life depicted in the film:

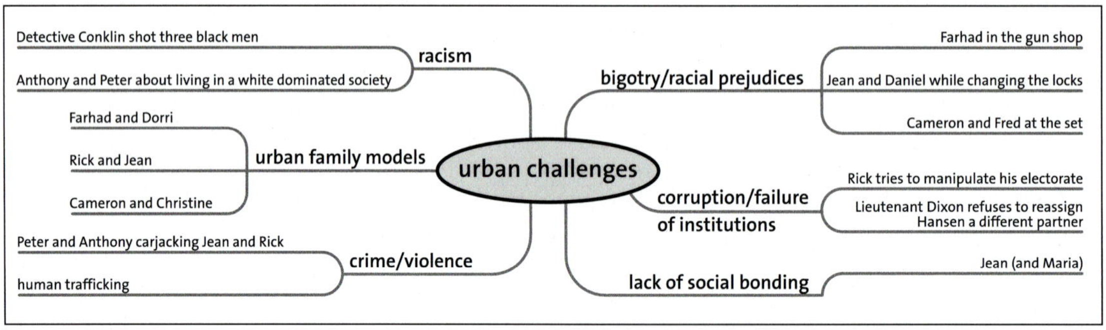

Impuls 3

individuelle Lösungen

Impuls 4

individuelle Lösungen

Component 1

Big city life in contemporary USA – introduction to plot and characters

Wie aus dem Titel zu schließen ist, spielt der Film im urbanen Raum von *Los Angeles,* der nach New York zweitgrößten Stadt der USA. Jedoch handelt es sich hierbei nicht wie im europäischen Sinne um eine Großstadt mit entsprechender Infrastruktur, sondern eher um eine Metropolregion, in der etwa 13 Millionen Menschen auf einer großen Fläche verstreut zusammenleben. Die Bedeutung von *Crash* im Film geht über die offensichtliche Konnotation hinaus: Es passieren zwar mehrere Autounfälle, wobei jedoch immer das Aufeinandertreffen verschiedener Charaktere mit unterschiedlichen soziokulturellen Hintergründen im Vordergrund steht. Hervorzuheben sind besonders die Themen *urban life (L.A., living together in a city), different ethnicities (multiculturalism, racism, conflicts)* und *crime (gun crime, carjacking).*

Ziel des Einstiegs ist es, die Erwartungen der Schüler an den Film abzurufen und mithilfe verschiedener Impulse Hypothesen zu möglichen Themen und Charakteren zu bilden. Als *pre-viewing activity* dient die ***Getting started*-Seite** (S. 3), welche der Klasse auf Folie präsentiert wird. Um die Aufmerksamkeit der Klasse auf die einzelnen Impulse zu lenken, ist es ratsam, zunächst nur den Titel, dann das DVD-Cover und schließlich die Zitate aufzudecken. Als differenzierende Maßnahme bietet es sich an, die Filmgenres anzugeben und die Schüler bestimmen zu lassen, welchen dieser Genres (Mehrfachnennungen sind möglich) sie die entsprechenden Impulse zuordnen würden.

1. What do title and DVD cover convey about the film in terms of genre and the characters that appear in it? What kind of film do you expect? Organize your ideas in a mind map.
2. On the basis of the quotes, speculate about possible topics of the film. Complete the mind map.

Die im Unterrichtsgespräch herausgearbeiteten Ergebnisse werden in Form einer Mindmap zusätzlich auf Folie festgehalten, damit im Verlauf der Unterrichtseinheit abgeglichen werden kann, inwieweit sich die Vermutungen bestätigen.

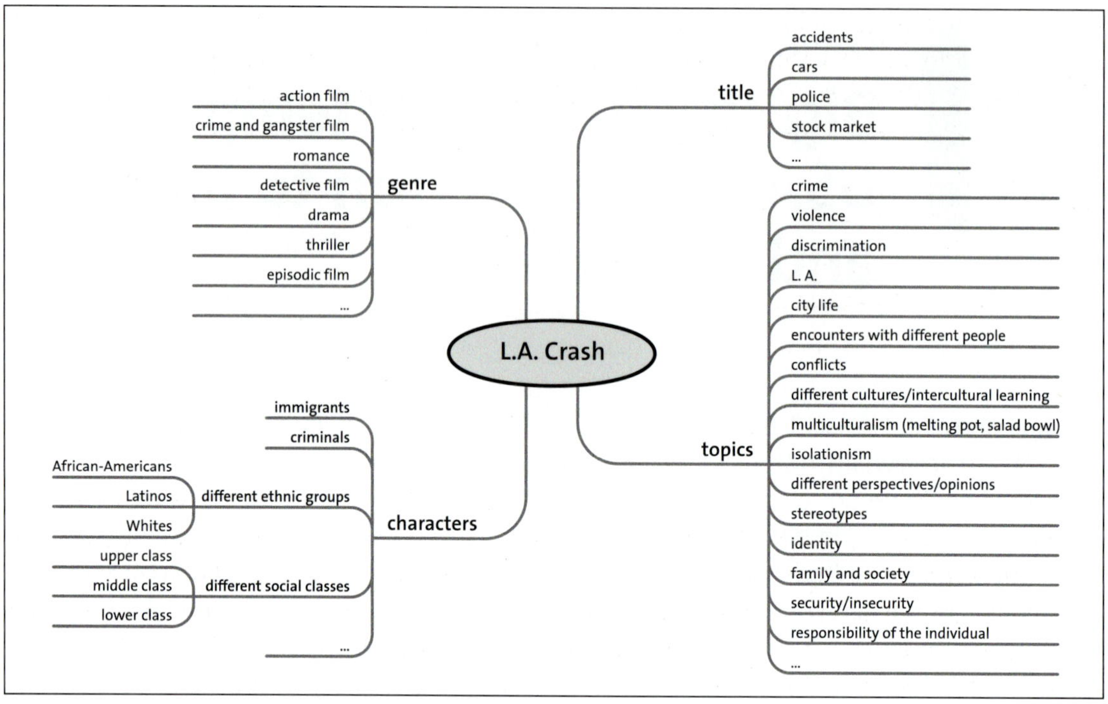

Um zu ermitteln, für welche Themen sich die Schülerinnen und Schüler am meisten interessieren, erstellen sie Rankings.

Which of these issues are you most interested in? Choose four topics and rank them accordingly.

Im Plenum wird dann ein Klassenranking erstellt, um die insgesamt vier beliebtesten Themen zu ermitteln. In einer *four-corner activity* werden anschließend die vier Spitzenreiter genauer definiert und Vermutungen bezüglich der Rolle im Film angestellt. Dazu werden die vier Themen den vier Ecken des Klassenzimmers zugeordnet.

Choose the topic (= discussion corner) you are most interested in. Tell your classmates why you are interested in this topic and speculate about how it might be illustrated in *L.A. Crash*. Decide on three important aspects to present in class after your discussion. Complete the mind map.

Entsprechend der Präferenzen der Schüler kann die Lehrkraft die *Components* thematisch auswählen beziehungsweise vertieft behandeln.

1.1 Survey of characters

L.A. Crash lebt vom Aufeinandertreffen verschiedener Charaktere und deren gegenseitiger Beeinflussung. Die Begegnungen und Herausforderungen verändern die Persönlichkeiten im Laufe des Films. Die Episodenstruktur verdeutlicht die verschiedenen Momentaufnahmen und lässt das wiederholte Aufeinandertreffen in veränderten Kontexten zu. Dies stellt die Schüler zugleich aber vor besondere Herausforderungen bezüglich der Charaktere und des Plots. Aufgrund der Episodenstruktur wird der Zuschauer permanent desillusioniert und muss bereits getroffene Einschätzungen zu einer Figur immer wieder revidieren. Viele Puzzleteile müssen also vom Zuschauer selbst zusammengesetzt werden, um ein Gesamtbild zu bekommen. Dies soll durch die *long-term-viewing task* (**Copy 1**, S. 41) erleichtert werden, indem die Schüler arbeitsteilig die unterschiedlichen Facetten der wichtigsten *Characters* während des ganzen

Films beobachten und sich dazu Notizen machen. Die *Copies* werden vor der Präsentation des Films ausgegeben. Der Lehrer teilt die Beobachtungsaufträge so zu, dass gleich viele Schüler für denselben *Character* zuständig sind. Da die Kopien mit Bildern und Namen versehen sind, können die Schüler die Figur, die sie beobachten sollen, problemlos identifizieren.

Concentrate on one character. While watching the film, continuously collect information. Write it down in the character sheet (*Copy 1*).

1. What do we know about the character?
2. Whom does he meet? Where? What happens?
3. Which challenges does the character face and how does he respond to them?
4. Which actions/reactions make him likeable/dislikeable?

Bewusst werden nicht nur Handlungen paraphrasiert, sondern auch komplexere Analyse- und Interpretationsfragen zu individuellen Herausforderungen gestellt. Außerdem wird die Empathie der Schüler gefördert, indem sie überlegen, welche Charakterzüge und Verhaltensweisen ihnen die Protagonisten sympathisch oder eher unsympathisch erscheinen lassen. Nach Sehen des gesamten Films werden die Ergebnisse zu Beginn des *Components 2* verglichen (Lösungsvorschläge zu *Copy 1*, S. 42ff.).

Nun rückt der Film selbst in den Fokus. Viele der mithilfe der *Getting-started*-Seite erarbeiteten Themen tauchen wieder auf: Das setting ist ein Tatort, welcher noch nicht genauer bestimmt wird, im Hintergrund ist die Stadt Los Angeles bei Nacht zu sehen. Tatsächlich werden auch gleich zu Beginn des Films die Implikationen des Titels bedient – so ist die Kollision des Dienstwagens des afroamerikanischen Ermittlers Graham Waters und seiner Partnerin Ria, einer Latina, mit dem Auto der Koreanerin Kim Lee nicht nur ein Unfall im eigentlichen Sinne. Dieser erste *crash* symbolisiert zugleich auch das Aufeinanderprallen verschiedener Ethnizitäten. Auf diese Themen konzentrieren sich die Schüler während des Schauens der ersten Szene (00:00:00 – 00:05:56). Dafür sind vor allem nonverbale Aspekte *(setting, actors, colour and lighting, …)* von Relevanz. Diese Art von Einstieg in den Film motiviert somit auch leistungsschwächere Schüler, da das Hörverstehen eine zweitrangige Rolle spielt.

1. While watching the first scene (00:00:00 – 00:05:56), mark all the topics in your mind map that you can find in the sequence. Add new topics.
2. Compare your findings with a partner.
3. One pair transfers their results to the transparency and presents them in class.

Da das Medium Film außer der Sprache auch Bilder übermittelt, wirkt es auf die Schüler motivierend. Um auch den leistungsschwächeren Schülern in den Folgestunden ein positives Filmerlebnis zu ermöglichen, sollen im darauf folgenden Unterrichtsgespräch Strategien für ein erfolgreiches Hör-/Sehverstehen erarbeitet werden.

1. Beside dialogues, there are other aspects that help you to understand the plot of the film, for example *setting, actors, colour and lighting*. Give examples of these aspects depicted in the first scene.
2. Which other strategies help you to understand a film in English?

Die Ergebnisse werden an der Tafel gesammelt und von den Schülern als Strategienrepertoire ins Heft übernommen.

Möglicher Tafelanschrieb:

1. Nonverbal aspects

nonverbal aspects	examples from the first scene
setting • city/landscape • decoration • props	big city in the background (skyline, lights), car crash/accident, police motorbike, police cars, crime scene tape
actors • body language (facial expression, gestures, movement) • costume/clothes • voice (volume, tone, intonation)	• the man looks serious, the woman looks confused, furious Asian woman • the man spots something in the bushes → his facial expression changes • policeman in uniform, the other man wears a suit and a coat → doesn't look like a policeman • aggressive tone → they argue
colour and lighting	dark colours/darkness → the scene takes place at night

2. Strategies to understand a film in English

- Hypotheses, suppositions and predictions on the basis of what I already know about the film help me to anticipate what could happen next.
- I concentrate on what I understand rather than on what I don't understand. I listen for keywords and write them down.
- I focus on the main plotline.
- I try to find out who the main characters are and collect information about them.
- I analyse the relation between the characters and draw conclusions about possible topics.
- I watch the film with English subtitles.

1.2 Relations of characters

In den darauffolgenden Szenen treffen verschiedene Personen unterschiedlicher ethnischer Gruppen aufeinander. Die Begegnungen sind gekennzeichnet durch Missverständnisse, Ignoranz, Stereotypisierung und Ablehnung. Die Afroamerikaner Peter und Anthony werden beispielsweise aufgrund ihrer Hautfarbe von der wohlhabenden weißen Staatsanwaltsgattin Jean Cabot als Kriminelle stigmatisiert. Die beiden bestätigen dieses Klischee umgehend, indem sie das Auto der Camerons rauben. In einer anderen Szene wird Shaniqua, Angestellte einer Versicherungsgesellschaft, von Officer John Ryan aufgrund ihres Namens, der häufig unter weiblichen Afroamerikanerinnen vorkommt, diskriminiert.[1]

[1] Im *Urban Dictionary* definiert ein Blogger den Namen folgendermaßen: „a common name used to mock/describe a black woman from the inner city. This name would include all of the stereotypes: long fake braids, big butt, ghetto voice." (http://www.urbandictionary.com)

Diese und weitere Aufeinandertreffen der Charaktere werden mithilfe von ***Copy 2*** (S. 48) analysiert. Durch das *guided viewing* wird das Hör-/Sehverstehen erleichtert, indem Charaktere aufgelistet und zentrale Zitate angeführt sind. Der Blick der Schüler wird so auf die wesentlichen Aspekte der Episoden gelenkt, was für die spätere thematische Betrachtung vorentlastend wirkt.

Read the quotes on *Copy 2*. While watching the following scenes, link the stills with the quotes and note down keywords to describe the context.

Es ist vor allem bei leistungsschwächeren Klassen ratsam, die DVD zwischendurch anzuhalten, damit ausreichend Zeit für Notizen zur Verfügung steht.

Compare and complete your findings with a partner. Note down open questions.

Das anschließende Plenumsgespräch dient der zentralen Ergebnissicherung und bietet die Möglichkeit, unbeantwortete Fragen zu klären. Dabei sollte besonders herausgestellt werden, dass alle Begegnungen durch Konflikte gekennzeichnet sind, die sich durch das Aufeinandertreffen von Menschen mit unterschiedlichen soziokulturellen Hintergründen ergeben.

What do we learn about the characters?
What do all encounters have in common?

Lösungsvorschlag zu *Copy 2* (S. 48):

 **a)** Jean and Rick Cabot	I am American citizen. I have right like you. I have right to buy gun.	**c)** Farhad at the gun shop after being stereotyped and insulted by the gun shop owner.
 **b)** John Ryan	We didn't get any coffee that you didn't want and I didn't order. And that's evidence of racial discrimination? Did you notice that our waitress was black?	**d)** Peter to Anthony after leaving an Italian restaurant in a "white" area where they had dinner. Peter seems to think that Anthony's "stereotype theory" is exaggerated.
 **c)** Farhad and Dorri	Looks like Detective Conklin shot himself the wrong nigger.	**e)** Graham to Ria, his partner, when they find the victim's wallet with his detective's badge under the front seat.
 **d)** Anthony and Peter	Shaniqua. Big fucking surprise that is.	**b)** Ryan to Shaniqua Johnson, a black HMO administrator, while calling her to ask for help for his ill father.
	And it was my fault because I knew it was gonna happen. But if a white person sees two black men walking towards her and she turns and walks in the other direction, she's a racist, right? Well, I got scared and I didn't say anything and 10 seconds later I had a gun in my face.	**a)** Jean Cabot to her husband Rick. She is afraid that the locksmith could sell the keys to gang members and that they might rob the Cabots like Anthony and Peter did.

 **e)** Graham Waters	I'm the goddamned district attorney in Los Angeles! If my car gets jacked, it's gonna make news. Fuck! Why did these guys have to be black?! I mean *why*? No matter how we spin this thing I'm either gonna lose the black vote or I'm gonna lose the law and order vote.	**a)** Rick Cabot to Karen, his assistant. He is concerned about his votes in the coming election after the carjacking by two black guys. He decides to award a black man to show his solidarity with the black population.

1.3 Characters in focus

Bei einer Polizeikontrolle fasst der weiße Polizist John Ryan die attraktive Christine unsittlich an. Ihr dunkelhäutiger Mann, Cameron, sieht Widerstand als zwecklos an und versucht, durch Gehorsam und Unterordnung eine Eskalation der Situation zu vermeiden. Officer Ryans Partner, der junge Officer Hansen, ist mit dem Verhalten seines Vorgesetzten überfordert und hält sich deshalb verunsichert zurück. Da die Szene inhaltlich sehr ergreifend ist, muss sie vorentlastet und intensiv nachbesprochen werden. Im Gegensatz zu den vorausgegangenen Filmszenen, in denen die Konflikte mit diskriminierendem Hintergrund verbal ausgetragen wurden, handelt es sich bei dieser Begegnung darüber hinaus um sexuelle Belästigung. Jedoch sollte diese nicht zu sehr in den Fokus der Analyse gerückt werden, da die Szene bei Schülern dieser Altersstufe Beklommenheit hervorrufen kann. Herausgearbeitet werden sollen vor allem die Charakterzüge der vier Protagonisten zu Beginn der Szene und kontrastiv dazu im zweiten Teil der Sequenz. So soll den Schülern bewusst gemacht werden, dass sich die Beurteilung von Personen bezüglich sympathisch/unsympathisch, *good guy/bad guy* situationsbedingt sehr schnell ändern kann.

Um besser reflektierte Ergebnisse zu erzielen, wird nach der Methode des Gruppenpuzzles vorgegangen. Nach dem Austeilen von ***Copy 3*** (S. 49) werden die Schülerinnen und Schüler dazu in vier Expertengruppen eingeteilt, welche je einem Protagonisten entsprechen.

Focus on one character.
Watch the first part (00:15:55–00:18:00) of the scene. Choose at least three suitable adjectives to describe your character.
Think about possible choices of action your character has in this situation and make notes.

Je nach Sprachniveau der Klasse ist es ratsam, zuvor die zur Auswahl stehenden Adjektive zu besprechen oder Wörterbücher zur Verfügung zu stellen. Leistungsstärkere Schülerinnen und Schüler können über die angebotene Auswahl hinaus Vokabeln einbringen. Anschließend findet ein Abgleich in den Expertengruppen statt.

Compare your results with the classmates that observed the same character.
Complete your notes (part 1 + possible choices).

Lösungsvorschlag zu *Copy 3* (S. 49), 1. Teil:

	Officer Ryan	Officer Hansen	Christine	Cameron
part 1	*self-confident* *arrogant* *impatient* *amused* *superior* *determined*	*cautious* *shy* *introverted* *tense*	*impulsive* *good-humoured* *outgoing* *extroverted* *smart* *defensive*	*kind* *polite* *optimistic* *relaxed* *trustworthy* *obedient*
possible choices	• accepts that they stopped the wrong people • arrests them • shoots Cameron because he feels threatened	• tries to intervene • lets his experienced colleague do it • calls colleagues to help him • shows solidarity with Christine and Cameron	• insults Officer Ryan • stays in the car	• is obedient, follows the instructions • gets angry and attacks Officer Ryan • gets back into the car and drives away

Im nächsten Schritt setzen sich die Arbeitsgruppen so zusammen, dass für jede Filmfigur ein Experte vorhanden ist. Gemeinsam wird überlegt, welches Verhalten die jeweiligen Personen nach diesem Aufeinandertreffen an den Tag legen werden. Dies wird kurz von den Schülern szenisch dargestellt werden. Die Klasse interpretiert die Vorführungen.

> Now get together in groups of four (for each character one expert). Present what you found out so far about the character. The other group members complete their worksheets.
>
> In a role play, act out how the scene might go on. You slip into the role of the character you observed before.
>
> Note down more choices of action in the chart when your classmates act out their versions.

Nachdem verschiedene Handlungsalternativen von den Schülern szenisch umgesetzt wurden, erfolgt der nächste Schritt im Plenum. Die Schüler werden mit dem tatsächlichen Verhalten der Charaktere in der zweiten Hälfte der Szene konfrontiert.

> Watch the second part (00:18:00–00:21:58) of the scene. Choose another three suitable adjectives to describe your character.

Im Unterrichtsgespräch wird anhand der Adjektive die Entwicklung der Charaktere im Verlauf der Szene nachgezeichnet. Dabei können die Adjektive in Tabellenform an der Tafel gesammelt werden, damit auch schwächere Schüler das Arbeitsblatt vervollständigen können.

> Describe your character in the first and in the second part of the scene. In how far does he/she change?
>
> How do the characters act/react and why? Is it morally justifiable to act in this way?

Lösungsvorschlag zu *Copy 3* (S. 49), 2. Teil:

	Officer Ryan	Officer Hansen	Christine	Cameron
	→ sexually harasses Christine	→ observes the scene; is shocked	→ first fights back, then endures what is happening, feels humiliated	→ tries to avoid the worst by being submissive
part 2	*unfriendly* *impolite* *bad-mannered* *mean, cruel* *rude, discourteous* *disgusting* *nasty, guilty*	*insecure* *confused* *irritated* *disgusted* *distressed*	*quarrelsome* *argumentative* *embarrassed* *annoyed* *angry, humiliated* *hurt* *disgusted*	*sincere* *obedient* *humiliated* *servile*

Abschließend werden im Unterrichtsgespräch die Rollenspiele dem vom Drehbuchautor gewählten Fortgang der Szene gegenübergestellt. Darüber hinaus wird die Szene mit den vorausgegangenen Szenen verglichen. Mögliche Fragen dazu sind:

Compare your staged versions of the scene to the movie. What is similar? What is different? Would you prefer one of your acted versions? Why (not)?

In how far is this scene realistic?

Compare this encounter of people in L.A. to the ones in the first scenes. What do they have in common? What is different?

Um die in der Stunde erarbeiteten Ergebnisse umzuwälzen und die Antizipationsfähigkeit der Schülerinnen und Schüler zu fördern, verfassen diese einen Tagebucheintrag aus der Perspektive eines der Protagonisten. Neben einer kurzen Zusammenfassung des Vorfalls sollen darin verschiedene Handlungsmöglichkeiten nach dem Ereignis angedacht werden.

Choose one character from the scene "Sobriety test". Write his or her diary entry. Summarize briefly what happened and think about possible actions you could undertake.

Die kreative Schreibaufgabe wird in der Folgestunde aufgegriffen.

Nachdem im vorausgegangenen Unterrichtsabschnitt die erste Begegnung zwischen Officer Ryan, Christine, Cameron und Officer Hansen bei einer Personenkontrolle im Fokus stand, war es die Aufgabe der Schüler, sich in die verschiedenen Charaktere hineinzuversetzen. In der kreativen Schreibaufgabe haben sie für eine der beteiligten Figuren in einem Tagebucheintrag die Gedanken zu den Geschehnissen festgehalten und mögliche Handlungsszenarien für die jeweilige Person entworfen.

Get together in groups with classmates that wrote the diary entry for the same character. Read the versions and decide on the best product to present in class.

Die gelungensten Tagebucheinträge werden in der Klasse vorgelesen. Um die Inhalte der übrigen kreativen Schreibaufgaben zusammenzuführen und ein Spannungsmoment über den Fortgang des Films aufzubauen, werden die in den Tagebucheinträgen beschriebenen Handlungsalternativen an der Tafel gesammelt.

Note down the alternative reactions of each character you mentioned in the diary entries on the blackboard.

Mögliches Tafelbild:

Officer Ryan	Officer Hansen	Christine	Cameron
• suborns Hansen not to report the incident • does not show any reaction at all because for him it was a usual police control • realizes that his behaviour was inappropriate and apologizes	• reports the incident • confronts Ryan with his behaviour • ignores the incident because Officer Ryan is his superior	• reports the incident to the police • blames Cameron for not having protected her • calls a newspaper to make her story public	• apologizes to Christine because he should have protected her • has a fight/ dispute with Christine • kills Ryan

Inwieweit die Schüler mit ihren Vermutungen richtig lagen, kann nun überprüft werden:

Let's find out how the characters really react after the sexual harassment by Officer Ryan. Make notes and compare your observations to the ideas on the board.

Dazu wird die Präsentation des Films fortgeführt (00:21:58–00:34:09). Die Schüler beobachten die Reaktionen: Christine will tatsächlich die Polizei anrufen, doch Cameron bringt sie davon ab, denn er meint, es habe sowieso keinen Zweck. Darauf folgt eine heftige Auseinandersetzung, in der sich beide gegenseitig vorwerfen, gar nicht zu wissen, was es wirklich bedeutet, Afroamerikaner zu sein. Dies deutet darauf hin, dass beide offenbar in sehr behüteten Verhältnissen aufgewachsen sind und Rassismus in ihren etablierten Kreisen bisher kaum eine Rolle gespielt hat. Officer Tom Hansen dagegen bittet seinen Chef, ihm einen anderen Partner zuzuweisen. Zwar hält dieser Ryan auch für einen Rassisten, jedoch wissen wir als Zuschauer gar nicht, ob Hansen ihm den genauen Tathergang geschildert hat. Der junge Polizist ist überrascht von der Reaktion seines Vorgesetzten, der selbst afroamerikanischer Abstammung ist, als dieser ihm eröffnet, dass er nur eine Alternative hat, nämlich allein auf Patrouille zu gehen.

All diese Figuren gehen unterschiedlich mit der Tat um: Christine empfindet sie als Demütigung ihres Mannes und als Degradierung; für Hansen handelt es sich um ein inakzeptables Dienstvergehen, was er nicht noch einmal miterleben möchte; Lieutenant Dixon sieht den Vorfall als Laune eines Untergebenen und Ryan selbst als Konsequenz seiner jahrelangen Arbeit als Polizist, die ihn verändert hat. Ob Ryans Verhalten also tatsächlich Folge seiner rassistischen Grundhaltung ist oder ob seine Reaktion vielmehr seiner individuellen momentanen Lage geschuldet ist, bleibt an dieser Stelle offen. Auch in unserer heutigen Lebenswelt sind die Probleme mit und unter ethnischen Minderheiten nicht mehr eindeutig und ausschließlich auf einen genuinen Rassismus zurückzuführen, sondern müssen immer im Kontext der individuellen Umstände gesehen werden.

Die Schüler tauschen sich nach dem Schauen des Filmabschnitts kurz mit dem Nachbarn aus.

How did the characters react after the incident? In how far do the reactions match with or differ from the options you mentioned in the diary entries? Which aspects put you on the right/wrong track?

1.4 Conflicts of characters – urban life as a challenge

Die folgende Filmsequenz zeigt ganz im Sinne der Episodenstruktur den weiteren Verlauf des Tages aus den verschiedenen Perspektiven der Charaktere, die mit den gesellschaftlichen Herausforderungen des Zusammenlebens in der Großstadt hadern. Dabei treffen sie in unterschiedlichen Konstellationen aufeinander. Als Daniel in Farhads Lebensmittelgeschäft ein Schloss austauscht, empfiehlt er ihm, die reparaturbedürftige Tür zeitnah komplett zu ersetzen. Farhad vermutet, dass Daniel mit diesem Ratschlag einen weiteren Auftrag an Land ziehen möchte, und reagiert unbeherrscht. Um die völlige Eskalation zu vermeiden, verlässt Daniel den Laden, ohne dass der uneinsichtige Farhad die ausgestellte Rechnung begleicht. Obwohl Ria und Graham intim miteinander sind, kritisiert sie, dass er jeden auf Distanz hält. Auslöser für ihre Meinungsverschiedenheit ist zwar die Tatsache, dass Graham während des Liebesspiels einfach ans Telefon geht und seiner Mutter dann auch noch erzählt, dass er gerade Sex mit einer Weißen habe. Enttäuscht zeigt sich Ria aber vor allem über Grahams Ignoranz, als er es mit der Bezeichnung ihrer ethnischen Abstammung nicht so genau nimmt; sie unterrichtet ihn darüber, dass sie keine Mexikanerin ist, sondern dass ihr Vater Puerto Ricaner ist und ihre Mutter aus El Salvador stammt. Auch Anthony belehrt Peter auf seine Weise, indem er ihm erklärt, dass die großen Fenster in öffentlichen Bussen den alleinigen Zweck hätten, die Insassen – überwiegend Afroamerikaner – besser sichtbar zu machen und sie so zu demütigen. Somit spielt Anthony hier nicht nur auf das mangelhafte öffentliche Verkehrsnetz in Los Angeles an. Das Haupttransportmittel der Menschen in Los Angeles ist das Auto. Seine Aussage ist natürlich auch als Anspielung auf die Bürgerrechtsbewegung der 1950er- und 1960er-Jahre zu verstehen, wo unter anderem durch Bus-Boykotte auf die Rassentrennung aufmerksam gemacht wurde.
All diese Szenen verdeutlichen, dass es nicht nur zu Konfliktsituationen zwischen Weißen und Schwarzen kommt, sondern dass die verschiedenen ethnischen Gruppen auch untereinander Schwierigkeiten haben und bestehende Stereotype übernommen werden. Farhad etwa scheint zu glauben, dass alle Latinos *amigos* in Gangs haben und sich gegenseitig Geschäfte zuschieben.

Als *pre-viewing activity* wird das bisher gesammelte Filmwissen aktiviert sowie die Antizipationsfähigkeit der Schüler gefördert, indem sie Vermutungen zum Kontext vorgelegter Filmzitate anstellen.

Speculate about which characters utter the following quotes and the contexts.

- "You try to cheat me, right? You have friend who fix door?"
- "My father is from Puerto Rico; my mother is from El Salvador. Neither one of those is Mexiko."
- "You have no idea why they put those great big windows on the sides of the buses, do you? One reason only: to humiliate the people of colour who are reduced to riding on it."

Die antizipierten und auch andere Aufeinandertreffen stehen im Mittelpunkt der *while-viewing task* auf ***Copy 4*** (S. 50). Während der Film fortgeführt wird (00:34:09–00:58:01), wählen die Schüler aus den Antworten jeweils das inhaltlich richtige Satzende aus.
Die behandelte Sequenz dient als Brücke zwischen den ersten Begegnungen der Charaktere und deren zufälligen oder geplanten Wiedersehen, wobei die Herausforderungen, die das

Großstadtleben an sie stellt, im Vordergrund stehen. Wenn bei leistungsstärkeren Klassen auf die szenenbezogene Überprüfung des inhaltlichen Verstehens verzichtet werden kann, ist es auch denkbar, ***Copy 4*** und ***Copy 5*** zugleich auszugeben, den Film am Stück bis zum Ende zu schauen und anschließend beide Arbeitsblätter zu besprechen.

Compare the worksheet with your neighbour's. If there are any unanswered questions about the sequence, note them down to ask in class.

Lösungsvorschlag zu *Copy 4* (S. 50):

Satz	1	2	3	4	5	6	7	8	9	10
Ergänzung	b	b	c	c	b	b	c	c	a	a

1.5 You always meet twice

In *L.A. Crash* begegnen sich innerhalb der dargestellten 36 Stunden einige der Charaktere ein zweites Mal – einige geplant, manche aus reinem Zufall. Nachdem Officer John Ryan Christine Thayer bei ihrem ersten Aufeinandertreffen sexuell belästigt und gedemütigt hat, rettet er ihr bei der zweiten Begegnung das Leben. Auch zwischen Cameron und Tom Hansen kommt es zu einem weiteren, zufälligen Wiedersehen, bei dem der junge Polizist Cameron wiedererkennt und sich schützend vor ihn stellt, als es fast zur Eskalation zwischen diesem und einem anderen Kollegen kommt. Ebenso treffen auch Farhad und Daniel wieder aufeinander, als der wutentbrannte Farhad vor dem Haus der Familie Ruiz auftaucht und durch Verkettung unglücklicher Umstände auf dessen Tochter Lara anstatt auf ihn schießt. All diese Begegnungen gehen glimpflich aus. Andere, wie etwa die zwischen Officer Hansen und Peter, haben fatale Folgen. In diesem *Component* stehen also die erneuten Begegnungen der Charaktere und deren Folgen im Vordergrund, bei denen die Zuschauer die Figuren von einer anderen Seite kennenlernen und Hinweise auf ihre Beweggründe bekommen. Diese Vorgehensweise des schrittweisen Entblätterns der Charaktere bewirkt die ständige Desillusionierung im Zuschauer – all seine Annahmen beziehungsweise Vorurteile erweisen sich immer wieder als unvollständig oder falsch, was eine endgültige Beurteilung der Figuren, wie etwa eine fixe Einordnung in Gut und Böse, bis zum Schluss verhindert. Am Ende steht für den Zuschauer die Erkenntnis, dass die Welt nicht endgültig beurteilt werden kann und Menschen nicht in Schubladen einzuteilen sind, sondern dass vom Einzelnen und den jeweiligen Umständen auszugehen ist.

Zum Einstieg in die letzte Phase der Filmpräsentation überlegen sich die Schüler, welche der Charaktere ihnen bisher am sympathischsten sind und für welche sie sich ein glückliches Ende wünschen. Sie spekulieren über mögliche Fortsetzungen der einzelnen Handlungsstränge: Finden Christine und Cameron wieder zueinander? Kann Detective Graham Waters seinen Bruder finden? Was plant Farhad? Wird er den Schlosser Daniel kontaktieren? Werden Anthony und Peter beim nächsten Autodiebstahl von der Polizei erwischt? Kann Jean ihre Krise beenden und ihre Wut ablegen? Findet Officer Ryan eine Lösung, seinem Vater zu helfen? Auf diese Weise wird die Antizipationsfähigkeit der Schüler gefördert. Im Plenum geben manche Schüler die Ergebnisse des Partnergesprächs wieder.

Before we watch the rest of the film, tell your partner for which of the characters you would like to see a happy ending and why. What could a happy ending for him/her be like?
Be ready to feedback to the class.

Das Anschauen des restlichen Films (00:58:01 – Ende) wird von einer offenen *guided viewing*-Aufgabe begleitet *(**Copy 5**,* S. 51*)*. Die Schüler ergänzen dabei Satzanfänge, wobei im Gegensatz zu *Copy 4* keine Antwortmöglichkeiten gegeben sind. Das Anforderungsniveau ist deshalb höher anzusiedeln. Je nach Leistungsstand der Klasse ist es ratsam, den Film zwischendurch kurz anzuhalten, um den Schülern die Möglichkeit zu geben, in Ruhe das Arbeitsblatt auszufüllen. Gelenkt durch das Arbeitsblatt beobachten die Schüler, wie sich die einzelnen Charaktere weiterentwickeln, welche Figuren sich ein zweites Mal begegnen und wie sie mit den Herausforderungen umgehen, die das Leben in der Großstadt an diesem Tag für sie bereithält.

Zur Ergebnissicherung werden Satzanfänge und -enden (diese können dem Lösungsvorschlag entnommen werden) auf Streifen an die Klasse verteilt. Die Schüler finden nun in einer *milling-around activity* den Partner, der den passenden Satzteil hat. Haben sich die Paare gefunden, werden die passenden Sätze im Plenum vorgelesen und der Kontext der Szene kurz erläutert.

Lösungsvorschlag zu *Copy 5* (S. 51):

1.	When Officer John Ryan crawls into the overturned car …
	… he recognizes Christine as the woman he molested the night before.
2.	Flanagan leaves Graham no choice: either he confirms that Detective Conklin shot his African-American colleague Lewis on racist grounds or …
	… his brother Peter will be arrested for life due to the Three-Strikes-Law.
3.	Hansen intervenes and defends Cameron because …
	… he recognizes Cameron from the incident the night before and wants to make up for his nonintervention.
4.	Before Cameron drops Anthony off …
	… he hands him back his gun and tells him that he embarrasses him and himself.
5.	What Farhad wants from Daniel is …
	... that he pays for what happened to Farhad and his shop.
6.	The bullet Farhad fires …
	… does not injure Daniel's daughter Lara because it is a blank cartridge.
7.	When they talk about music, Tom Hansen doubts that …
	… Peter likes to listen to country music.
8.	When Peter reaches into his pocket, Tom …
	… thinks that he will pull out a gun and instinctively shoots him.
9.	Graham's mother blames him for …
	… Peter's death because he has not found his brother and she thinks that he doesn't care about his family anymore.
10.	Farhad tells Dorri that …
	… Lara is his little angel who saved him.
11.	After talking to Rick on the phone, Jean …
	… hugs her housekeeper Maria telling her that she actually is her best friend.
12.	Although Lucien, the mechanic, has offered him a large sum of money for the illegal aliens, Anthony …
	… decides to release them and even gives them some money to buy food.

Long-term-viewing activity: character sheet

☐ 
Graham Waters
(Don Cheadle)

☐ 
Anthony
(Chris "Ludacris" Bridges)

☐ 
John Ryan
(Matt Dillon)

☐ 
Tom Hansen
(Ryan Phillipe)

☐ 
Cameron Thayer
(Terrence Howard)

☐ 
Farhad
(Shaun Toub)

Some facts about …

- **Age:**
- **Profession:**
- **Ethnicity:**
- **Social status:**
- **Family:**
- **Else:**

Whom does your character meet?
Where?
What happens?

Which **challenges** does he face?
How does he respond to these challenges?

Does this character appeal to you?
Which actions/reactions/characteristics make him **likeable/dislikeable**?

Character sheet for Graham Waters (possible solution)

Some facts about …
• **Age:** – in his thirties • **Profession:** – L.A. police detective – his partner is Ria • **Ethnicity:** – Afro-American • **Social status:** – middle class • **Family:** – his mother Louise (addicted to drugs) – his younger brother Peter (criminal) – his girl friend (?) Ria

Whom does your character meet? **Where? What** happens?	**scene of crime**: when he and his partner Ria arrive at the scene of the crime they are involved in an accident; the accident makes Graham reflect upon life in the city: "In LA, nobody touches you – always behind this metal and glass. Think we miss that touch so much, that we crash into each other just so we can feel something." **on a parking lot**: Graham and Ria were called to investigate the murder of a black colleague **in Graham's bedroom**: although Graham is having sex with Ria he answers the phone; they start a fight **at Louise's house**: Graham visits his drug-addicted mother; she wants to know if he found his brother; when he sees that her fridge is empty, he brings her groceries **in the district attorney's conference room**: Flanagan blackmails Graham **at the hospital**: Graham and his mother came to see Peter's dead body; Louise blames Graham for his brother's death
Which **challenges** does he face? How does he respond to these challenges?	• when Ria reproaches him for his ignorance about her origin, he plays it down • Graham's mother is addicted to drugs – he seems to look in on her every now and then and he answers every phone call from his mother; however, he does not seem to take any further action in order to help his mother • when Flanagan asks him to keep silent about the money that was found in the black colleague's car, Graham finally plays along to save his criminal brother from a long term of imprisonment
Does this character appeal to you? Which actions/ reactions/ characteristics make him **likeable/ dislikeable?**	• the way he talks to his mother on the phone while having sex with Ria makes him less likeable (he hurts both his mother and Ria) • him ignoring the fact that Ria is not Mexican makes him less likeable • the fact that he looks in on his drug-addicted mother, holds her hand, listens to her and buys groceries for her makes him seem to be a caring son and thus more likeable • Graham takes his job very seriously and first does not want to give in to Flanagan's extortion, but when he realizes that his brother Peter would have to bear the consequences, he finally tells the district attorney what he wanted to hear: Detective Conklin shot a black colleague for racist reasons; the audience understands that he wants to protect his brother and spare his mother's feelings → this makes him likeable • when Louise blames Graham for his younger brother's death and tells him that Peter has bought some groceries for her just before he died, she hurts Graham's feelings: he feels guilty but he has bought the groceries for her; he does not tell this to his mother and also doesn't mention what he knows about Peter's criminal actions → the audience feels compassion for Graham • in the end, we feel pity for him: he comes back to the place where his brother was shot and finds his statuette

Character sheet for Anthony (possible solution)

Some facts about …
• **Age:** in his twenties • **Profession:** gangster (steals cars) • **Ethnicity:** African-American • **Social status:** lower class • **Family:** ? his best friend is Peter • **Else:** very talkative

Whom does your character meet? **Where? What** happens?	**in the street**: after a dinner at an Italian restaurant, Anthony and his friend Peter steal Rick Cabot's car **in the stolen car**: while talking about music, Anthony and Peter run over an Asian man **at Lucien's garage**: Peter and Anthony want to sell Rick's car to Lucien but he does not want to have it as it has Choi's blood on it **in the street**: Anthony does not greet one of his black neighbours because he is convinced that he steals from black people **in the street**: Anthony and Peter want to carjack Cameron's car; but he defends his car; when the police appears, Anthony hides in the car while Cameron gets off and confronts them **at Lucien's garage**: Anthony wants to sell Choi's van to Lucien, but they discover illegal aliens in the back of the car
Which **challenges** does he face? How does he respond to these challenges?	• when Anthony realizes that a white woman acts as if she was afraid of him and Peter because they are black, he decides to carjack her and her husband's vehicle – they threaten them with their guns and steal their car • when Anthony and Peter run over an Asian man, Anthony first wants to leave him there, but then he listens to his friend Peter and the two of them drop Choi in front of a hospital • when Anthony is in the car with Cameron, they do not speak until Cameron drops him off; Anthony seems to be surprised that he is handed back his gun; he does not protest when Cameron tells him that he finds him embarrassing; he has broken with one of his own rules, namely not to steal from blacks • Anthony does not accept Lucien's offer to buy the persons that he found in Choi's van; he releases them in the street
Does this character appeal to you? Which actions/ reactions/ characteristics make him **likeable/ dislikeable?**	• Anthony is angry about the way blacks are treated; however, with his actions he confirms some existing stereotypes and clichés; his dialogues with Peter are rather witty, which makes the audience laugh about him and his partner Peter • although he is a criminal and threatens people with his gun, he does not harm anybody; but the aggressive tone during those assaults makes him less likeable • for the first time he does not seem to know what to say when he is in the car with Cameron – this experience does not stop him from stealing cars for Lucien; but when he refuses to sell the illegal aliens to Lucien and releases them in the streets of L.A., it seems as if he wanted to right his wrongs → this makes him more likeable

Character sheet for John Ryan (possible solution)

Some facts about …
• **Age:** in his forties • **Profession:** police officer Tom Hansen's partner • **Ethnicity:** white • **Social status:** middle class • **Family:** lives with his ill father his mother left his father • **Else:** racist

Whom does your character meet? **Where? What** happens?	**phone call**: Ryan calls the Health Maintenance Organization (HMO) (Shaniqua) to ask for help for his father who suffers from a urinary infection; Shaniqua cannot help him immediately **police check**: Ryan stops Cameron and Christine and harasses her sexually **at home**: at night, Ryan cares for his father who is in pain because of his urinary infection **at the HMO**: Ryan visits Shaniqua to ask her for a proper treatment for his father; first he is humble but as Shaniqua cannot help him, he insults and discriminates against her again **parking lot, police station**: Hansen tells Ryan that he has been reassigned; Ryan: "You think you know who you are? You have no idea!" **car crash**: Ryan rescues Christine **at home**: Ryan again cares for his father; he seems to be more pensive
Which **challenges** does he face? How does he respond to these challenges?	**phone call**: Shaniqua cannot help him immediately → failure of institutions (healthcare system) → feeling frustrated and helpless, Ryan insults her because of her stereotypical name **police check**: Christine (African-American!) doesn't obey → Ryan wants to show her who is superior by degrading her and Cameron **at home**: Ryan has to care for his father because the HMO cannot offer the required treatment → Ryan tries to comfort his father without really being able to help him **at the HMO**: as Shaniqua cannot help him, Ryan again shows his frustration by insulting her **parking lot, police station**: Ryan is confronted with the consequences of his behaviour → he wants to justify or explain his behaviour **car crash**: he's again confronted with his inappropriate behaviour in the past → he risks his life to rescue the woman he harassed before
Does this character appeal to you? Which actions/ reactions/ characteristics make him **likeable/ dislikeable?**	• cares for his father → likeable • insults Shaniqua → he is a racist • the audience clearly disapproves of Ryan's behaviour at the police control → he is absolutely dislikeable • he is desperate because he cannot help his father → makes him likeable • he again shows his racist attitude → makes him dislikeable • the fact that he tries to give reasons for his behaviour shows his insecurity/despair • Ryan surprisingly turns into a (kind of) hero

Character sheet for Tom Hansen (possible solution)

Some facts about …
• **Age:** – about 30 years old • **Profession:** – police officer – John Ryan's partner – rather new in the job • **Ethnicity:** – white • **Social status:** – middle class • **Family:** – no information • **Else:**

Whom does your character meet? **Where? What** happens?	**police control**: Cameron + Christine; his partner Officer Ryan harasses Christine sexually **at Lt. Dixon's office**: Hansen wants Dixon to assign him a new partner; Dixon refuses because he is afraid of losing his job but at the same time accuses Ryan of racism **parking lot, police station**: he tells Ryan that he has been reassigned; Ryan: "You think you know who you are? You have no idea!" **police control**: Anthony and Peter want to carjack Cameron's car; Peter gets into the car; the police stops Cameron and Peter; Hansen recognizes Cameron and lets him off with a warning **hitch-hiking**: Hanson gives Peter a lift to the city centre; he mistakenly assumes that Peter wants to get a gun out of his pocket and therefore shoots him **in the outskirts**: Hansen burns his car to destroy all evidence
Which **challenges** does he face? How does he respond to these challenges?	**police control**: Hansen is aware of the inappropriate behaviour of his partner but at the same time doesn't want to/dare to undermine his authority → Hansen is stunned, confused, passive, obedient, doesn't intervene **at Lt. Dixon's office**: • Hansen avoids the conflict with Ryan and therefore wants to be assigned a new partner • Hansen is "lost in the system of politics, hierarchy and racial oppression" **police control**: Hansen wants to compensate for his misbehaviour the day before **hitch-hiking**: when Hansen realizes that he shot Peter in error, he is paralyzed; he leaves the dead body at the side of the street; as he cannot deal with the situation, he burns his car presumably to delete his past
Does this character appeal to you? Which actions/ reactions/ characteristics make him **likeable/ dislikeable?**	• his personal appearance is likeable ("nice guy") • the fact that he seems to feel helpless arouses sympathy • the fact that he doesn't intervene makes him less likeable • he faces his moral duty in a certain way • the fact that he wants to compensate for his inappropriate behaviour makes him an upright person • led by stereotypes, he reacts in a wrong way and makes a terrible mistake → sympathy

Character sheet for Cameron Thayer (possible solution)

Some facts about …
• **Age:** in his forties • **Profession:** film director • **Ethnicity:** African-American • **Social status:** upper middle class • **Family:** his wife is the attractive Christine, also an African-American • **Else:** rather polite and obedient

Whom does your character meet? **Where?** **What** happens?	**police control in the street**: they are stopped by Ryan and Hansen; his wife is harassed sexually by Officer Ryan **in the bedroom**: Christine accuses him of not defending her; Christine wants to report the incident to the police, Cameron keeps her from doing it **at the set**: Fred, the producer, wants him to take the scene again because the black actor didn't talk "black enough"; Cameron first pretends not to understand what he means but then agrees **lunch break**: Christine comes to the set to talk to Cameron and apologizes for her behaviour the evening before; he leaves her behind **police control**: Anthony and Peter want to carjack Cameron's car (curious incident because they didn't expect a black driver); Peter gets into the car; the police stops them; Cameron is in a fury and provokes one of the policemen; Hansen lets him off with a warning **in the street, at night**: Cameron stops next to Hanson's burning car to enjoy the moment; Christine calls; Cameron tells her that she loves him
Which **challenges** does he face? How does he respond to these challenges?	**police control in the street**: Cameron is confused but obedient; he doesn't dare to revolt against the police and wants to avoid an even more serious conflict **in the bedroom**: Cameron, himself embarrassed by the police, doesn't see any chance of justice; he defends himself because from his perspective there was no alternative to react **at the set**: by stereotyping the black actor, Fred indirectly discriminates against Cameron as well → instead of defending himself, he obeys **lunch break**: Cameron neither wants to talk to Christine nor deal with the incident **police control**: it's a similar situation to the one at the beginning of the film; this time Cameron reacts aggressively because he feels unjustly treated as first his car was carjacked and then he was treated like a criminal, although he actually was the victim **in the street, at night**: Cameron wants to become reconciled with Christine
Does this character appeal to you? Which actions/ reactions/ characteristics make him **likeable/ dislikeable?**	• the fact that he doesn't defend his wife makes him less likeable • his reserved behaviour makes him generally likeable • he seems to be sorry for Christine but cannot show it emotionally • as he shrinks from a conflict the second time, he appears to be little self-confident or overtaxed • the audience sympathizes with Cameron because he's again the victim confronted with the challenges of a multi-cultural city (racism, crime) • the phone call illustrates Cameron's warm-hearted side

Character sheet for Farhad (possible solution)

Some facts about …

- **Age:**
  in his fifties
- **Profession:**
  shop owner
- **Ethnicity:**
  Persian immigrant
  → American citizen
- **Social status:**
  lower/middle class
- **Family:**
  – his daughter Dorri (a nurse)
  – his wife Shereen
- **Else:**
  he doesn't read English, his spoken English is faulty some-times; Dorri translates for him

Whom does your character meet? **Where? What** happens?	**in the gun shop**: Farhad wants to buy a gun; when the gun shop owner calls him Osama, he's furious about this insult; Dorri intervenes and finally buys the gun without Farhad **in Farhad's shop**: a locksmith repairs the lock because the door doesn't close; the locksmith advises him to replace the door; Farhad assumes that the locksmith wants to cheat on him and insults him **in Farhad's shop, the next morning**: Farhad enters the shop and finds it ransacked; he calls the locksmith's company because he wants to find out the locksmith's name; he suspects him to be behind the break-in; the insurance adjuster tells Farhad and Dorri that the insurance will not cover the damage as Farhad did not replace the door, although the locksmith told him to do so **backyard of the shop**: Farhad finds the bill with the locksmith's name (Daniel Ruiz) **in front of Daniel's house:** Farhad wants to take revenge on Daniel; when Daniel comes home from work, Farhad wants Daniel to pay for the damage; as Farhad loses control, he fires a bullet at Daniel; right at this moment, his daughter Lara jumps into his arms but she's not shot dead **in Farhad's shop**: Farhad tells Dorri about the incident; as Dorri takes the gun and the bullets, she detects that they aren't bullets but blanks
Which **challenges** does he face? How does he respond to these challenges?	**in the gun shop**: Farhad is stereotyped because of his language; he reacts aggressively and insists on his right to buy a gun as he's an American citizen **in Farhad's shop**: as the door needs to be closed during the night, he's dependent on the locksmith; Farhad feels betrayed and thus overreacts **in Farhad's shop, the next morning**: Farhad is furious about the break-in and feels abandoned and betrayed by everyone; he decides to take revenge on the one responsible for his misery **in front of Daniel's house**: although Farhad didn't want to fire the bullet at Daniel's daughter, it seems as if he shot an innocent girl; Farhad himself is shocked about his deed **in Farhad's shop**: still holding the gun in his hand, Farhad has to tell Dorri what happened; Farhad has to cope with his deed; he calls Lara his little angel who saved him (supposedly from killing Daniel); he attributes the happy ending to Lara, not to himself
Does this character appeal to you? Which actions/ reactions/ characteristics make him **likeable/ dislikeable?**	• his reaction is understandable although he's rather aggressive • as the locksmith is a very likeable person and tries to help him, Farhad's overreaction reflects badly on his character • Farhad seems to recognize his overreaction lead by wrong convictions; he's shattered

Characters and quotes (00:05:56–00:15:55)

- **Who says what to whom in which context? Link the stills with the quotes and write down keywords that describe the situation.**
- **What do we learn about the characters?**
- **What do all encounters have in common?**

a) Jean and Rick Cabot

b) John Ryan

c) Farhad and Dorri

d) Anthony and Peter

e) Graham Waters

I am American citizen. I have right like you. I have right to buy gun.	
We didn't get any coffee that you didn't want and I didn't order. And that's evidence of racial discrimination? Did you notice that our waitress was black?	
Looks like Detective Conklin shot himself the wrong nigger.	
Shaniqua[1]. Big fucking surprise that is.	
And it was my fault because I knew it was gonna happen. But if a white person sees two black men walking towards her and she turns and walks in the other direction, she's a racist, right? Well, I got scared and I didn't say anything and 10 seconds later I had a gun in my face.	
I'm the goddamned district attorney in Los Angeles! If my car gets jacked, it's gonna make news. Fuck! Why did these guys have to be black?! I mean *why*? No matter how we spin this thing I'm either gonna lose the black vote or I'm gonna lose the law and order vote.	

[1] stereotypical name for an African-American woman

Choices

Focus on one character:

1. Watch the first part (00:15:55–00:18:00) of the scene. Choose at least three suitable adjectives to describe your character.
2. Think about possible choices of action your character has in this situation and write them down (keywords).
3. Get together in groups of four (for each character one expert). In a role play, act out how the scene might go on. Note down more choices of action in the chart when your classmates act out their version.
4. Watch the second part (00:18:00–00:21:58) of the scene. Choose another three suitable adjectives to describe your character.

extroverted *impolite* *introverted* *optimistic* *superior*
disgusted *disgusting* *confused* *argumentative*
insecure *self-confident* *embarrassed* *rude* *humiliated*
sincere *distressed* *guilty* *mean*
impulsive *polite* *good-humoured* *amused* *kind*
hurt *servile* *irritated* *angry*
impatient *shy* *discourteous* *quarrelsome* *unfriendly*
obedient *bad-mannered* *relaxed* *cruel*
defensive *smart* *arrogant* *outgoing* *trustworthy*
cautious *tense* *annoyed* *nasty* *determined*

	Officer Ryan	Officer Hansen	Christine	Cameron
part 1				
possible choices				
part 2				

Understanding the scenes (00:34:09–00:58:01)

Tick (✓) the correct answer.
Note: there isn't a task for every episode.

1	**Farhad thinks that Daniel …**
a	doesn't want to have money because he didn't repair the lock.
b	wants to recommend somebody to him who sells doors.
c	is unable to fix the lock.

2	**Lucien, the mechanic, tells Anthony and Peter about a show on the Discovery channel …**
a	to prove to them that he is not stupid.
b	to explain to them how easy it is to identify a stolen car.
c	to make fun of some people who do not know why they are arrested.

3	**Ria is disappointed with Graham because …**
a	he calls her a white woman.
b	he tells his mum about her.
c	he thinks that she is Mexican.

4	**When Rick asks his assistant Karen about the crime, she …**
a	confirms that the crime was racially motivated.
b	tells him that there are a dozen witnesses.
c	admits that they don't know if the police-man and the victim knew each other.

5	**Anthony doesn't greet the man walking by …**
a	because he doesn't like thieves.
b	because he thinks that it is wrong to steal from your own people.
c	because he thinks that it is wrong to steal purses from old ladies.

6	**Anthony argues that …**
a	bus prices in L.A. should be reduced.
b	people of colour are reduced to riding the bus.
c	taking the bus reduces a black man's pride.

7	**John Ryan tries to convince Shaniqua Johnson that his dad needs to see another doctor by …**
a	apologizing to her for his behaviour when he called her.
b	telling her that there is no better qualified person for her job.
c	telling her that his father was one of the first employers who paid equal wages to black people.

8	**Christine comes to see Cameron at the set …**
a	because she wants him to apologize.
b	to tell him she felt humiliated.
c	to apologize for what she said.

9	**The insurance company would pay for the damage …**
a	if Farhad had replaced the door.
b	if Farhad had told the locksmith to fix the lock.
c	if Farhad had replaced the lock.

10	**When Ryan wishes Hansen good luck, he also wants …**
a	to explain to him that their job makes people change.
b	to tell him that they will work together again after a few years.
c	to show him that he doesn't really know himself.

How to cope with the challenges (00:58:01 – end)

Complete the following sentences.
Note: there isn't a sentence for every scene.

1.	When Officer John Ryan crawls into the overturned car …
2.	Flanagan leaves Graham no choice: either he confirms that Detective Conklin shot his African-American colleague Lewis on racist grounds or …
3.	Hansen intervenes and defends Cameron because …
4.	Before Cameron drops Anthony off …
5.	What Farhad wants from Daniel is …
6.	The bullet Farhad fires …
7.	When they talk about music, Tom Hansen doubts that …
8.	When Peter reaches into his pocket, Tom …
9.	Graham's mother blames him for …
10.	Farhad tells Dorri that …
11.	After talking to Rick on the phone, Jean …
12.	Although Lucien, the mechanic, has offered him a large sum of money for the illegal aliens, Anthony …

Component 2

Lives colliding

L.A. Crash lebt vom Aufeinandertreffen verschiedener Charaktere und deren gegenseitiger Beeinflussung. Die Episodenstruktur reiht viele einzelne Momentaufnahmen aneinander, was die Schüler vor besondere Herausforderungen bezüglich der Charaktere und des Plots stellt. Viele Puzzleteile müssen vom Zuschauer selbst zusammengesetzt werden, um ein Gesamtbild zu bekommen. Bereits getroffene Einordnungen von Figuren und deren Handlungen müssen revidiert oder ergänzt werden. Anhand der *long-term-viewing task (**Copy 1**,* S. 41*)* aus *Component 1* stellen die Schüler zu Beginn des zweiten *Components* die Entwicklung der ausgewählten Protagonisten dar und analysieren deren Wirkung auf den Zuschauer.
Darüber hinaus werden in *Component 2* ausgewählte Szenen genauer betrachtet. Die Wege einiger Figuren kreuzen sich im Handlungsverlauf ein zweites Mal. Wie der Ladenbesitzer Farhad und der Schlosser Daniel oder der junge Polizist Tom Hansen und der Regisseur Cameron Thayer treffen auch Christine Thayer und der Polizist John Ryan erneut aufeinander. Diese Wiederbegegnung soll stellvertretend sowohl inhaltlich als auch kinematografisch analysiert werden.
Um die Porträts der dargestellten Familien nachzuzeichnen sowie Leerstellen interpretatorisch zu füllen, werden die familiären Situationen der Staatsanwaltsgattin Jean Cabot, des Schlossers Daniel und der drogenabhängigen Louise Waters genauer beleuchtet.
Für die vertiefte Arbeit mit dem Film kann den Schülern das *fact sheet* ***Copy 6*** (S. 61) ausgeteilt werden, auf dem die wichtigsten filmischen Mittel aufgeführt sind. Auf das Infoblatt kann im Verlauf der Unterrichtseinheit bei Bedarf immer wieder zurückgegriffen werden.

2.1 Role identity of characters

Durch die Interaktion mit verschiedenen Mitmenschen – mit Fremden und Familienmitgliedern – ergeben sich Konstellationen, in denen die Protagonisten unterschiedliche soziale Rollen einnehmen. So ist Graham Waters beispielsweise nicht nur Ermittler und John Ryan nicht nur Polizist, beide sind auch besorgte Söhne, die sich (der eine weniger, der andere mehr) um ein leidendes Elternteil kümmern. Die Episodenstruktur des Films beeinflusst auch die Sympathielenkung der Zuschauer, da die Figuren in den verschiedenen Szenen unterschiedlich agieren. So werden weitere Facetten ihres Charakters sichtbar beziehungsweise Hintergründe bekannt, die das Verhalten der Akteure erklären oder nachvollziehbar machen. Als *long-term-viewing activity* haben die Schüler während der Präsentation des Films *(Component 1)* die sechs facettenreichsten Protagonisten beobachtet: Der Zuschauer lernt Graham Waters zunächst als gedankenverlorenen, etwas übermüdeten Ermittler der Polizei in Los Angeles kennen, der aufgrund seines Verhalten gegenüber seiner Partnerin Ria und seiner Mutter oberflächlich und arrogant erscheint. Sein distanziertes Verhalten erschließt sich dem Zuschauer besser, als er bei seiner Mutter vorbeischaut, denn diese lebt allein, ist drogenabhängig und kaum in der Lage, sich um sich selbst zu kümmern. Dieser Zustand scheint ihn zu belasten, aber er redet mit niemandem, auch nicht mit Ria, über seine familiären Verhältnisse. Eine weitere schwierige Situation resultiert aus seiner Ermittlungsarbeit, als er von Flanagan, dem etwas schmierigen PR-Mann von Staatsanwalt Rick Cabot, erpresst wird. Er soll als Mordmotiv an einem schwarzen Polizisten Rassismus angeben, obwohl die Indizien gegen diese Lesart sprechen. Schließlich hat er aber keine Chance, sich Flanagan zu widersetzen: Entweder er erzählt die erwünschte Version vom rassenfeindlichen Mord (die es Rick Cabot ermöglicht, einen weißen Polizisten hinter Gitter zu bringen und so vom Diebstahl seines Autos durch zwei Schwarze abzulenken) oder aber sein krimineller Bruder Peter kommt für 15 Jahre ins Gefängnis.[1] Vermutlich erkennt Waters in dieser Situation, dass er das seiner Mutter nicht antun kann, und spielt notgedrungen mit. Spätestens als sein Bruder tot aufgefunden wird und seine Mutter ihm die Schuld daran gibt, wird klar, dass auch er verletzlich ist.

Anthony ist Peter Waters Freund. Er ist aufgeweckt, redegewandt und philosophiert gerne über verbreitete Klischees und Stereotypen zwischen Schwarzen und Weißen, um sie auch selbst immer wieder zu bestätigen. Zusammen mit Peter stiehlt er Autos, wie etwa das von Rick und Jean Cabot, um sie dann an den Hehler Lucien zu verkaufen. Als es den beiden nicht gelingt, den Wagen des erfolgreichen, aber psychisch angeschlagenen afroamerikanischen Regisseurs Cameron Thayer zu stehlen, schweigt Anthony zum ersten Mal und widerspricht auch nicht, als Cameron sagt, wie beschämend er sein Verhalten findet. Wohl von sich selbst enttäuscht, weil er seine selbst aufgestellte Regel, keine anderen Schwarzen zu bestehlen, fast gebrochen hätte, aber auch weil ihn Camerons Worte getroffen haben, zeigt er am Ende seine gute Seite, indem er die Asiaten, die Lucien im geklauten Transporter entdeckt, nicht verkauft, sondern sie auf der Straße freilässt.

John Ryan erleben wir zunächst als rassistischen Widerling, der bei einer Polizeikontrolle zu weit geht, als er Christine, die Frau des erfolgreichen schwarzen Regisseurs Cameron Thayer, in dessen Beisein sexuell belästigt. Auch Shaniqua Johnson, die für die HMO arbeitet, wird Ziel seiner rassistischen Beschimpfungen. Jedoch hat John Ryan auch andere Seiten. Als liebevoller Sohn kümmert er sich nach Feierabend um seinen an starken Schmerzen leidenden Vater. Er fühlt sich machtlos gegenüber den strengen Regeln des Gesundheitssystems, die seinem Vater eine weitere Untersuchung verwehren. Zum Helden wird er, als er Christine Thayer das Leben rettet.

Während John Ryan vordergründig den *bad cop* verkörpert, scheint sein junger Kollege Tom Hansen auf dem besten Weg zu sein, ein *good cop* zu werden. Dieser hat ein ausgeprägtes Gerechtigkeitsempfinden. Zwar verrät er seinen Kollegen John nach der sexuellen Belästigung nicht, beantragt aber bei seinem Vorgesetzten einen Partnerwechsel. Die Worte, die ihm Ryan mitgibt, als er sich von ihm verabschiedet („You think you know who you are? You have no idea."), erweisen sich als Prophezeiung. Auch er ist nicht frei von Vorurteilen, was den Zuschauern und ihm selbst auf drastische Weise deutlich wird, als er die Bewegung des Afroamerikaners Peter, der etwas aus seiner Hosentasche holen möchte, missinterpretiert und ihn im Affekt erschießt.

Cameron Thayer ist ein erfolgreicher Regisseur, der Konflikte zu vermeiden versucht, indem er sich nachgiebig zeigt. Sein defensives Verhalten bei der Polizeikontrolle stellt seine Ehe auf die Probe, denn seine Frau Christine wirft ihm vor, er habe sich demütigen lassen. Dieser Konflikt löst eine regelrechte Identitätskrise in ihm aus; er fährt mit seinem Auto durch die Stadt, um über alles (seine Ehe? seine Herkunft? seinen Status? seine Reputation?) nachzudenken. Dabei macht er unfreiwillig Bekanntschaft mit den Autodieben Anthony und Peter und beweist Mut, als er sich nicht geschlagen gibt und sein Auto vor den beiden Ganoven verteidigt. Als er später der Polizei gegenübersteht, begegnet er zum zweiten Mal dem jun-

---

[1] Das 1994 in Kalifornien eingeführte *"Three Strikes and You're Out"-Law* ermöglicht es den Richtern, einen Kriminellen nach seiner dritten Straftat zu lebenslanger Haft zu verurteilen. Dabei ist die Schwere dieses dritten Vergehens unbedeutend. Das Gesetz betrifft ethnische Minderheiten unverhältnismäßig stark – über 45 % der Inhaftierten, die auf der Grundlage des *Three Strikes Laws* zu lebenslanger Haft verurteilt werden, sind Afroamerikaner. (http://www.law.stanford.edu/organizations/programs-and-centers/stanford-three-strikes-project/three-strikes-basics)

gen Officer Hansen. Dieser glaubt, genau zu verstehen, warum Cameron so verstört ist. Er schämt sich für den jungen Anthony, der nichts aus seinem Leben macht. Am Ende des Films wird ihm bewusst, dass er in seinem Leben einiges erreicht hat und seine Frau liebt.
Farhad, der aus Persien stammende Ladenbesitzer, begegnet fast allen Menschen mit Misstrauen und vermutet hinter jedem einen Betrüger, wodurch alle Begegnungen mit ihm durch einen aggressiven Ton gekennzeichnet sind und es unweigerlich zur Konfrontation mit ihm kommt. Er wird vom Besitzer des Waffenladens als Jihadist beschimpft, was er sich nicht gefallen lässt und lautstark betont, dass er als amerikanischer Bürger das Recht dazu habe, eine Waffe zu kaufen. Kurzerhand wird er von einem Sicherheitsmann aus dem Laden geworfen, aber seine Tochter Dorri, die ihm immer beisteht und bei Bedarf übersetzt, schließt den Waffenkauf ab. Auch als der aus Mexiko stammende Schlosser Daniel Farhads Türschloss austauscht, ihm aber nahelegt, die Tür vollständig ersetzen zu lassen, vermutet Farhad sofort das abgekartete Spiel einer Latino-Bande, die sich gegenseitig Geschäfte zuschanzen. Daniel versteht die Beschuldigungen nicht und verlässt den Laden, ohne dass Farhad die Rechnung begleicht. Als nachts tatsächlich eingebrochen wird, beschließt Farhad, sich an Daniel zu rächen, und schießt mit seiner neu erworbenen Waffe auf Daniels kleine Tochter Lara. Dies löst eine Wandlung in Farhad aus. Da die Waffe nur mit Platzpatronen geladen war, ist dem kleinen Mädchen nichts passiert; Farhad fühlt sich erlöst und sieht in Lara seinen kleinen persönlichen Engel. Zurück in seinem Laden überreicht er seiner Tochter Dorri die Waffe und bittet sie, diese mitzunehmen. Seine Einstellung kann dadurch erklärt werden, dass er es als Einwanderer vermutlich besonders schwer hatte, seine Träume zu verwirklichen. Zahlreiche Enttäuschungen und Betrugsfälle könnten der Grund dafür sein, dass er allen Menschen misstrauisch begegnet.

Um die während des Films gesammelten Ergebnisse abzugleichen, tragen die Schüler, welche dieselbe Figur beobachtet haben, in Kleingruppen ihre Erkenntnisse zusammen und diskutieren, wann sie die Handlungen der Figur als nachvollziehbar empfanden und wann sie eher unsympathisch auf sie wirkten. Sie veranschaulichen ihre Ergebnisse mithilfe einer Sympathiekurve, indem sie die verschiedenen Ereignisse auf einem Spektrum von *likeable* bis *dislikeable* so miteinander verknüpfen, dass man auf einen Blick erkennen kann, wie sich ihre Haltung gegenüber der Figur im Laufe des Films verändert hat (siehe Lösungsvorschlag zu *Copy 7*; exemplarisch John Ryan, S. 63). Da sich die Eindrücke der Gruppenmitglieder sicherlich unterscheiden, muss ein Konsens gefunden werden, damit das Gruppenergebnis begründet werden kann (***Copy 7***, S. 62).

Get together in groups with students who observed the same character. First compare your results and, if necessary, complete your notes (*Copy 1*).

To sum up your findings, draw a line that indicates in which situations you found the character rather likeable and in which situations you found him dislikeable. Be ready to present your results in class (*Copy 7*).

Nach einer kurzen Stellungnahme, in der ein Schüler der jeweiligen Gruppe der Klasse den Verlauf ihrer Sympathielinie erklärt, werden die Kopien als Poster im Klassenzimmer aufgehängt. Abschließend erstellen die Schüler mit Klebepunkten ein Ranking, welche der sechs Figuren ihnen insgesamt am sympathischsten und am wenigsten sympathisch scheint.

Present your results in front of the class. After the presentations, rank the characters according to their likeability.

Die Lösungsvorschläge zu *Copy 1* auf S. 42 ff. sind detaillierte Darstellungen der Charaktere, die von den Schülern so ausführlich nicht erwartet werden können. Sie dienen vor allem dem Lehrer als Orientierung, sodass möglichst unterschiedliche Aspekte abgedeckt sind.

2.2 Meeting again – from bully to hero?

In *L.A. Crash* begegnen sich innerhalb der dargestellten 36 Stunden einige der Charaktere ein zweites Mal. So stellt sich zum Beispiel der junge Polizist Tom Hansen schützend vor Cameron, als er diesen wiedererkennt. Er verhindert so, dass es zwischen einem weiteren Polizisten und Cameron zur Eskalation kommt. Ebenso treffen auch Farhad und Daniel wieder aufeinander, als der wutentbrannte Farhad vor dem Haus der Familie Ruiz auftaucht und durch Verkettung unglücklicher Umstände auf dessen Tochter Lara anstatt auf Daniel schießt. All diese Begegnungen gehen glimpflich aus, andere, wie etwa die zwischen Officer Hansen und Peter, haben fatale Folgen. In diesem Unterrichtsabschnitt stehen also die (Wieder-)Begegnungen der Charaktere und deren Folgen im Vordergrund.

Zu den Personen, die in *L.A. Crash* ein zweites Mal aufeinandertreffen, gehören auch Officer John Ryan und Camerons Frau Christine. Während der Polizist Christine und ihren Ehemann bei einer Personenkontrolle gedemütigt hat, wird er bei seiner zweiten Begegnung mit Christine zu deren Lebensretter. Im Film werden die Gründe für Christines Unfall nach ihrem Besuch bei Cameron am Set nicht deutlich: Ist es Zufall oder wollte sie sich umbringen, nachdem Cameron sie abgewiesen und nach Hause geschickt hatte? Jedenfalls ist es die sprichwörtliche Ironie des Schicksals, dass ausgerechnet Officer John Ryan, *bully* und Auslöser für die Ehekrise der Thayers, zum selbstlosen Lebensretter seines ursprünglichen Opfers wird. Doch nicht nur seine Tat lässt ihn für Christine und die Zuschauer in einem anderen Licht erscheinen. Auffallend ist vor allem die Darstellung Ryans, denn die eingesetzten filmischen Mittel wecken Assoziationen mit der Darstellung der „Heroes of 09/11". So weist das rote Feuerwehrauto und der blaue Himmel im Hintergrund nicht nur auf die Farben der amerikanischen Flagge hin, auch die Darstellung des Helfers am Ort der Katastrophe (hier: des Unfalls) erinnert sehr stark an die Berichterstattung nach dem Terroranschlag. Durch diese Überstilisierung erscheint Officer Ryan eher als tragischer Held.
Um die Schüler auf die genaue Bildbetrachtung einzustimmen und ihnen den Bezug zu der Heldendarstellung in den amerikanischen Medien zu verdeutlichen, werden als Einstieg zwei sehr ähnliche Fotos verwendet, wobei eines als *Still* dem Film entnommen und das andere ein Pressefoto der Anschläge des 11. Septembers ist. In einer *lend-me-your-eyes activity* beschreiben die Schüler sich paarweise jeweils das andere Bild, welches der Partner vorerst nicht sehen darf. Basierend auf den Beschreibungen sollen Gemeinsamkeiten und Unterschiede der Fotos herausgearbeitet werden. Im nächsten Schritt, jetzt sehen die Schüler beide Fotos, werden diese in ihrer Wirkung auf den Betrachter analysiert. Die Schüler diskutieren im *double circle* (alle Partner A im *inner circle,* alle Partner B *im outer circle)* mit wechselnden Gesprächspartnern die Frageimpulse von ***Copy 8*** (S. 64).

Mögliche Antworten zu *Copy 8* (S. 64), tasks 2–4:

In both pictures we can see a man in uniform (police/firefighter) in the foreground. Both are there to help and rescue people. In the background you can see some scene of destruction or accident indicated by a fire engine/smoke. Due to the smoke in both pictures, the background seems to be slightly blurred. While the firefighter is still in action, shouting and pointing somewhere (giving directions to someone?), the police officer is looking rather exhausted and a little bit sad. Maybe he has already accomplished his task.

The saying is that a picture can express much more than you can explain with words. Both pictures express more than they show. We can deduce more information from them because we know these kinds of pictures that show heroes at work: they were all over the world after the terror attacks on the WTC in 2001.

The director uses this visual language, not to remind his viewers of 09/11, but to depict Officer John Ryan as a typical American hero. It's striking that the colours of the picture allude to the star-spangled banner.

Nachdem die Schüler für die im Film verwendete Bildsprache sensibilisiert wurden, stellt sich die Frage, warum der Regisseur Paul Haggis Officer Ryan in der nun folgenden Szene zum Helden stilisiert:

To concentrate on the images more easily, we are going to watch the scene without sound. Concentrate on what you see and summarize what happens in the scene.

Im nächsten Unterrichtsschritt wird die Szene *Car Crash* (00:58:01 – 01:03:52) ohne Ton vorgeführt. Nach dem Sehen fassen die Schüler in Partnerarbeit die Szene zusammen.

Direkt im Anschluss bearbeiten die Schüler in Einzelarbeit ***Copy 9*** (S. 65). Sie füllen die *thought bubbles* aus und formulieren so die Gedanken der Protagonisten bei ihrer dramatischen zweiten Begegnung. Zur Ergebnissammlung dieser Aufgabe werfen sich die Schüler einen Ball zu und lesen ihre Idee zum entsprechenden Moment vor. Wie bei einem Blitzlicht werden so relativ spontan die Ideen ins Plenum geworfen – sie müssen nicht weiter kommentiert werden.

Anhand des letzten *Screenshots* auf ***Copy 9*** (S. 65) soll abschließend im Unterrichtsgespräch geklärt werden, ob sich Christines Meinung über Officer Ryan geändert hat:

Is Ryan Christine's hero?
Can you forgive what he did to her because he saved her life?
How does this scene change the viewer's opinion about Officer Ryan?

Wenn ausreichend Zeit zur Verfügung steht, kann die Szene nun mit Ton noch einmal geschaut werden.

2.3 Family portraits – functional and dysfunctional relationships

Die Protagonisten im Film *L.A. Crash* bilden sich ein Urteil über andere Personen, ohne diese genau zu kennen. Die Bilder, die sie sich von ihren Mitmenschen machen, basieren auf Momentaufnahmen und Verhaltensweisen, die von Misstrauen, Vorurteilen und Unsicherheit geprägt sind. Lediglich der Zuschauer erhält Einblick in das Privatleben mancher Figuren und kann aufgrund der familiären Hintergründe Rückschlüsse auf Verhalten und Denkweisen der Protagonisten ziehen. Die verschiedenen Episoden von *L.A. Crash* zeichnen dabei unterschiedlichste Familienporträts: Neben scheinbar intakten und von starkem Zusammenhalt geprägten Familien, wie etwa die von Daniel, finden sich auch Beispiele dysfunktionaler familiärer Beziehungen wie die zwischen Inspector Graham Waters und seiner drogenabhängigen Mutter Louise. Ein Teil der persönlichen Geschichten, die darauf hindeuten, wie es zu den unterschiedlichen Familienverhältnissen gekommen ist, wird durch die filmische Bildsprache erzählt. Zwar lenkt diese den aufmerksamen Zuschauer, lässt ihm aber auch Raum für eigene Interpretationen.
In diesem Unterrichtsabschnitt arbeiten die Schüler zunächst heraus, wie die familiären Situationen filmisch dargestellt werden. In Form eines Rollenspiels versetzen sich die Schüler dann in die Charaktere hinein, greifen so auf kreative Weise die Implikationen der filmsprachlichen Mittel auf und füllen darüber hinaus die inhaltlichen Leerstellen. Dieser kreative und empathische Ansatz soll Aufschluss darüber geben, inwieweit äußere Faktoren den persönlichen Lebensweg und das Familienleben bestimmen können.

Alle in *L.A. Crash* porträtierten Familien werden vom Leben in der Großstadt beeinflusst; sie werden von Begegnungen mit fremden Menschen geprägt. Damit die Schüler beurteilen können, inwiefern es sich bei den folgenden Szenen um funktionale oder dysfunktionale familiäre Verhältnisse handelt, definieren sie zunächst ihr eigenes Konzept einer perfekten Familie.

What is a perfect family in your eyes?

Der Einstieg in das Thema "family" erfolgt somit global und zugleich mit persönlichem Bezug. Die Schüler machen sich zunächst in Einzelarbeit Gedanken zur Impulsfrage *(Think!)*, bevor sie sich mit einem Partner austauschen *(Pair!)*. In der darauffolgenden Phase *(Share!)* diskutieren die Partner mit einem weiteren Zweierteam zusätzliche Impulsfragen:

Does a happy and successful family life depend on where you live?
Are rural families happier than urban families?

Im nachfolgenden Unterrichtsgespräch fassen die Schüler die Ergebnisse ihrer Diskussionsgruppen zusammen.

Im nächsten Schritt arbeiten die Schüler anhand von drei exemplarisch ausgewählten Szenen heraus, wie unterschiedliche Familien in der Großstadt Los Angeles im Film dargestellt werden. Sie beurteilen, inwieweit sich diese Darstellungen mit ihren eigenen Vorstellungen eines perfekten Familienlebens decken beziehungsweise sich von ihnen unterscheiden *(**Copy 10**, S. 67)*.

In the film *L.A. Crash* we get to know different urban families. While watching the following scenes, fill in the grid on the worksheet (*Copy 10*) and answer the questions.

Anhand von Requisiten und Soundeffekten arbeiten die Schüler heraus, was die Filmsprache zusätzlich zur gesprochenen Sprache über die Familiensituation und das Verhalten der Familienmitglieder verrät. Zur genaueren Analyse der kinematografischen Mittel empfiehlt es sich, die Szenen im verzögerten Modus zu schauen oder sie zwei Mal zu zeigen. Dazu kann auch erneut das *fact sheet* ***Copy 6*** (S. 61) herangezogen werden.

Lösungsvorschlag zu *Copy 10* (S. 67):

	Scene 1 (00:24:25–00:29:24)	**Scene 2** (00:41:55–00:42:27)	**Scene 3** (00:48:25–00:58:20)
Title	**Family as a haven**	**Unhappy**	**The happy days are gone**
a) Who? Where? What? Why? When?	• Daniel and his daughter Lara in Lara's room • Lara is hiding under her bed because she heard a bang and thought it was a bullet coming through her window	• Maria, the housekeeper, comes back from taking young James Cabot to school • She tells Jean, who apparently just got up, that her car didn't work and that she didn't want James to take his huge plastic toy to school	• Graham and his mother Louise at Louise's house (living room, terrace, kitchen) • Graham visits his mother, helps her to stand up and lays her on the sofa

	• Daniel tries to comfort Lara, telling her the story of his invisible and impenetrable cloak that a fairy gave him on his fifth birthday; he pretends to put the cloak around her neck • Lara buys Daniel's story and goes back to bed • evening/night; after work	• Jean does not pay any attention to what Maria is telling her; she only slams the dish-washer door and reprimands Maria for not having put the clean cups into the cabinet • while Maria stays behind puzzled, Jean goes upstairs in the morning	• Louise takes Graham's hand, cries, asks twice whether he found his brother • Graham opens Louise's refrigerator and sees that there is almost nothing in it • day time (about lunch time?)
b) Context of the film	• Daniel comes home from two difficult jobs: first he exchanged some locks for a rich family and was mistaken for a gang member by Jean Cabot; then a Persian shop owner thought he wanted to cheat on him • this scene takes place the night before Farhad, the Persian shop owner, threatens him with a gun	• Jean had an argument with her husband Rick because she wants the locks to be changed again as she does not trust the Latino locksmith • the tone of their argument was quite aggressive • before she falls down the stairs	• Ria asked Graham to apologize for the way he spoke to his mum when she called him on the phone while he was having sex with Ria • while Graham is inside, Ria is waiting in the car • Graham lies to Ria, pretending that his mother was not at home
c) Cinematic devices	• **props:** Lara's room is lovingly decorated with animal posters, blankets, pillows and cuddly toys • **lighting:** the lamps close to Lara's bed give off a soft (yellowish), warm light • **sound:** – quiet music – Daniel and Lara don't speak very loudly; they almost whisper – the beep of Daniel's pager just after he closes the door from the outside; the hip hop music that begins to play in this scene → Lara's room seems to be a sanctuary; almost like a fairy world and a contrast to the loud and dark world that exists outside her room	• **props:** – James' plastic toy (and in a later scene his teddy bear) are the only signs of his existence; we do not see him – Jean is in her dressing gown → she has only just woken up	• **props:** the pictures on the piano show a young couple (pre-sumably Graham's parents); a soldier (Graham's dad?); a family with two boys, one of them a baby (Graham's family?); the same couple (now older, in their forties), a boy in an American football dress → show that there were happy family days in the past – on the table: a bent rusty spoon, a syringe and a used piece of tin foil → these are Louise's drug paraphernalia → in contrast to what we see in the pictures, Louise is not happy anymore; one of her sons and her husband are absent; she is ill

d) Perfect family life?	Daniel and his wife Elizabeth try to create a safe environment for Lara to grow up in. Daniel takes Lara's concerns very seriously. His family seems to be Daniel's haven – here he is sensitive and soft; he is not confronted with any prejudices.	James does not seem to play a very important role in Jean's life as we never see him; Jean seems to be too preoccupied with herself; there are also some implications about Rick cheating on his wife with his assistant Karen. The Cabots don't seem to be a happy family.	Apparently Louise cannot be left alone. She seems to feel abandoned by her sons and her husband. This is not a working family anymore.

Während des Schauens machen sich die Schüler Notizen. Nach dem Abgleich mit einem Partner können verschiedene Schüler ihre Ergebnisse auf Folie präsentieren, die im Unterrichtsgespräch durch den Rest des Kurses ergänzt werden.

2.4 Speculating on the reasons for dysfunctional relationships

Die drei ausgewählten Szenen werfen einige Fragen auf: Warum ist Louise drogenabhängig? Warum sind ihre Söhne so unterschiedlich und was hat zu ihrem Auseinanderleben geführt? Warum musste Daniel mit seiner Familie umziehen? Was wünscht sich Daniel für seine Familie? Welche Rolle spielt Familie in Jeans Leben? In diesem Unterrichtsabschnitt beantworten die Schüler diese Fragen bei einer *talk show* und zeichnen somit die Lebensgeschichte der drei Figuren nach. Der Lehrer leitet über:

> In *L.A. Crash* we are not told everything about the different families. However, some cinematic devices underline and/or reveal some more information about the action. In a talk show some of you will act out what Louise Waters, Daniel Ruiz and Jean Cabot can tell about themselves and about their family lives.

Jean Cabot wird im Film als frustrierte, wohlhabende Ehefrau dargestellt, die dauernd gereizt ist, den Auslöser dafür aber nicht kennt. Ihr Mann, der Staatsanwalt Rick Cabot, arbeitet viel und scheint ihr nicht die Aufmerksamkeit zu geben, die sie braucht. Eine gewisse Distanzierung und Leere ist in ihrem Eheleben zu beobachten. Darüber hinaus gibt es mehrere Hinweise darauf, dass Rick eine Affäre mit seiner Assistentin Karen haben könnte. Auch Jeans Sohn James wird immer nur erwähnt, taucht aber nie im Film auf, was verdeutlicht, wie sehr Jean mit sich selbst beschäftigt ist. Es ist vor allem die Haushaltshilfe Maria, die sich um den Jungen kümmert. Als Jean die Treppe hinunterstürzt und sich dabei den Knöchel verstaucht, muss sie feststellen, dass sie einsam ist und nicht einmal Freunde hat, die für sie da sind. Jean sehnt sich nach sozialer Nähe und nimmt in ihrer Verzweiflung ihre Haushälterin Maria in den Arm, die einzige Person, die immer da ist, aber dafür bezahlt wird.

Daniel, ein Schlosser, der aus Mexiko stammt, ist ständig mit dem Vorurteil konfrontiert, Mitglied einer Latino-Gang zu sein. Tatsächlich geht er jedoch einem geregelten Arbeitsleben nach und sorgt für seine Familie. Damit seine Tochter sicher aufwachsen kann, ist er mit seiner Familie in eine bessere Gegend gezogen, weg von Gewalt und Verbrechen. Er arbeitet hart, damit sie sich dieses Leben leisten können, und erträgt deshalb Beschimpfungen schweigend.

Was Louise Waters in ihre Situation gebracht hat, lässt sich anhand der Bilder auf dem Klavier erahnen. Sie zeichnen ein Porträt einer heilen Familie: Louise mit ihrem Mann und den beiden Kindern Graham und Peter. Konnte sie den Verlust ihres Ehemanns nicht verkraften? Hat sie sein Tod oder sein Verschwinden in die Drogenabhängigkeit getrieben? Warum ist

der ältere Sohn Graham Polizist geworden, wohingegen sein jüngerer Bruder von zu Hause abgehauen ist und sich als Krimineller durchschlägt?
Drei Schüler bereiten anhand der *role cards* (**Copy 11**, S. 68) und mithilfe der herausgearbeiteten Implikationen im Film die Familiengeschichte ihrer Figur vor. So füllen sie auf kreative Weise die Leerstellen des Films, indem sie sich überlegen, welche Ereignisse, Begegnungen und Entscheidungen die Protagonisten in die aktuelle Situation gebracht haben könnten. Währenddessen notieren sich die übrigen Schüler der Klasse Fragen, die sie diesen Figuren gerne stellen würden:

For the students who will act out one of the characters:
With the help of the role cards and the worksheet (*Copy 11*), put yourselves into your character's position.

For the rest of the class:
Write down questions you want to ask about their families. Try especially to examine aspects that don't become clear in the film.

Die drei Schüler, die sich als Louise, Daniel und Jean präsentieren, setzen sich der Klasse gegenüber. Der Lehrer bettet die *talk show* in einen Kontext ein, woraufhin sich die Personen zunächst vorstellen und dann die Fragerunde beginnt.

Welcome to our talk show *Big City Life L.A.* To today's show with the topic "Families in Focus" please welcome our guests: Louise Waters, Daniel Ruiz and Jean Cabot. Will you quickly introduce yourselves and then answer our audience's questions about your family lives?

Im Anschluss an die Fragerunde sollte allen Schülern die Gelegenheit gegeben werden zu bewerten, ob die Antworten der *guests* wahrscheinlich sind.

Do you think this was a probable version of Louise's/Daniel's/Jean's life? Why (not)?

Zur Sicherung der Ergebnisse und zur Vertiefung der in *Component 1* und *2* behandelten Aspekte kann an dieser Stelle der folgende Schreibauftrag als Hausaufgabe gestellt werden:

All the re-encounters in *L.A. Crash* tell us that you cannot really judge another person.
Comment on this aspect by referring to at least two characters in the film. (about 200–300 words)

Die Aufarbeitung der Ergebnisse erfolgt in der darauf folgenden Stunde über einen *homework check,* bei dem die Schüler einige Texte ihrer Mitschüler lesen und dann dem Nachbarn weitergeben. Dabei notieren sie sich fünf interessante Aspekte.

Read some of your classmates' texts. Note down 5 aspects you read about in your classmates' texts.

Film/movie terminology (fact sheet)

Field size		Camera positions	
	**long shot:** people or objects shown from a long distance away		**establishing shot:** shows location at the start of the scene
	**full shot:** shot from a middle distance showing whole body or object		**overhead shot:** bird's-eye view; shot from directly above a scene to give an overview and also focus on specific events
	**medium shot:** character's upper body or part of an object can be seen		**over-the-shoulder shot:** shot over the shoulder of a character to show what he/she can see in the scene
	**close-up:** focuses on head and shoulders; importance of facial expression		**reverse-angle shot:** shot from the opposite side; shows a dialogue partner or what a character can see in the background without turning around (e.g. through use of mirrors)
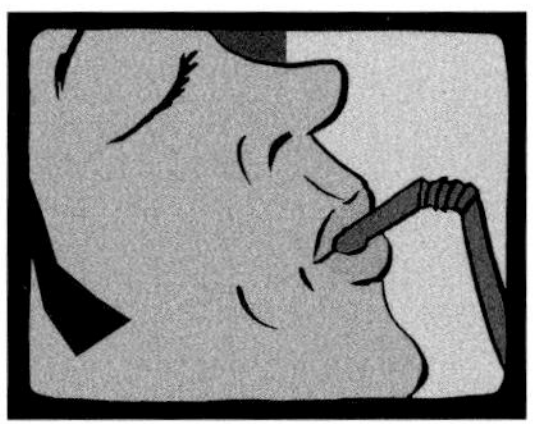	**extreme close-up:** shows only a part of an object or face, especially the eyes or mouth; gives a very detailed impression of the character's emotional state		**camera angles** 1 **high-angle:** shot from above 2 **eye-level:** shot from a horizontal perspective 3 **low-angle:** shot from below
	**camera movements** **tracking:** the camera itself moves and follows a moving object or person		
	**pan:** camera moves from side to side from a stationary position **tilt:** movement up or down from a stationary position		

Focus on characters: ______________________

According to the chronology of situations in which the character appears, draw a line that indicates in which situations you found him more likeable and in which situations you could not understand his actions or found him dislikeable.

What happens? (chronology of events)	
likeable ☺  dislikeable ☹	

Focus on characters: Officer John Ryan (possible solution)

According to the chronology of situations in which the character appears, draw a line that indicates in which situations you found him more likeable and in which situations you could not understand his actions or found him dislikeable.

What happens? **(chronology of events)**	**phone call:** Ryan calls Shaniqua Johnson of the HMO; he insults her on the phone	**police check:** Ryan stops Cameron and Christine and uses his superior position to sexually harass Christine in front of her husband	**at home:** Ryan cares for his father and helps him: it hurts him to see his father suffer	**at the HMO:** Ryan is there to achieve a better treatment for his father; he apologizes to Shaniqua, tells his father's life story; but when Shaniqua tells him that she cannot do anything for his father, he becomes insulting again	**car crash:** Ryan rescues Christine Thayer after a car accident, risking his own life
	he seems to be a racist (phone call and police check)				
likeable ☺ **dislikeable** ☹	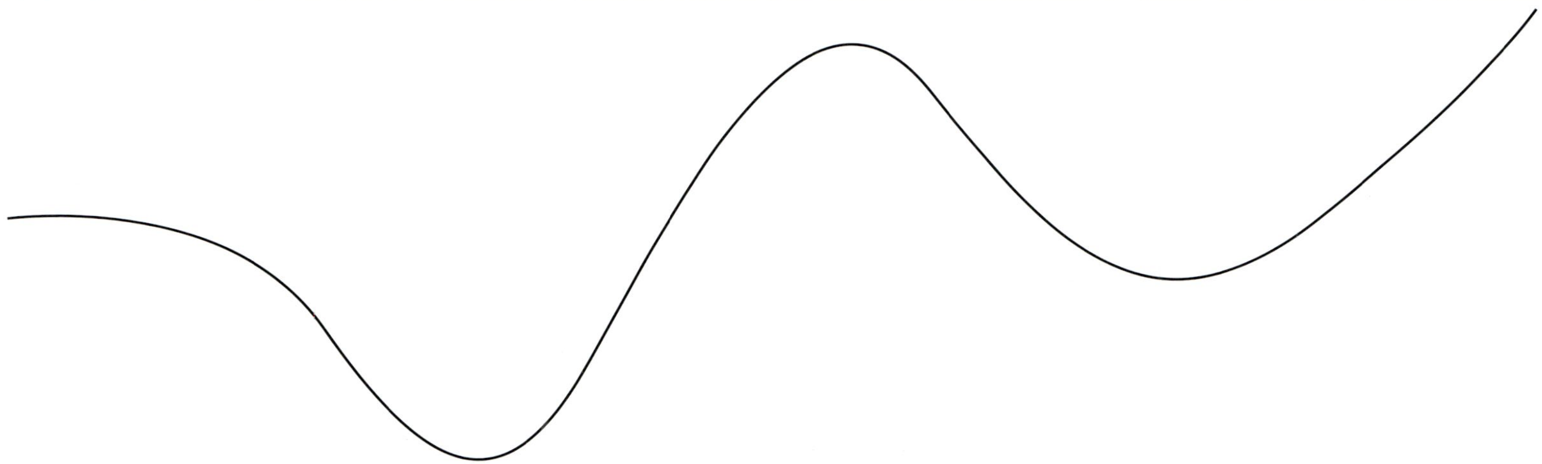				

Lend me your eyes

"A picture is worth a thousand words"

Partner A

1. Describe the picture to your partner without showing it to him/her. Point out details.
2. What do the pictures have in common?
3. "A picture is worth a thousand words." Explain this saying referring to the pictures. What do they make you think of?
4. What might have been the director's intention?

Useful phrases
- In my picture you can see …
- On the left/right there is/are …
- In the foreground/background/centre …
- What strikes the eye is …
- We can assume that …
- The facial expression can best be described as …
- The viewer has the impression that …
- The photo reminds me of …
- The photographer/director wants to express/show/emphasize …

✂- -

"A picture is worth a thousand words"

Partner B

1. Describe the picture to your partner without showing it to him/her. Point out details.
2. What do the pictures have in common?
3. "A picture is worth a thousand words." Explain this saying referring to the pictures. What do they make you think of?
4. What might have been the director's intention?

Useful phrases
- In my picture you can see …
- On the left/right there is/are …
- In the foreground/background/centre …
- What strikes the eye is …
- We can assume that …
- The facial expression can best be described as …
- The viewer has the impression that …
- The photo reminds me of …
- The photographer/director wants to express/show/emphasize …

From bully to hero?

**What is Officer John Ryan/Christine Thayer thinking in these scenes?
Write down your ideas in the thought bubbles.**

From bully to hero? (possible solution)

What is Officer John Ryan/Christine Thayer thinking in these scenes? Write down your ideas in the thought bubbles.

Oh my God!
This woman needs help! I have to get her out as soon as possible!
The gas could ignite any second!
I shouldn't lose time …

Oh no! Please no!!
This can't be true – it is this creep again. I don't want him to help and touch me! No!!
I'd rather want to die in here!
Why does this have to happen to me????

It's the director's wife.
No time for regret nor excuses.
Calm down, John!
You became a policeman to help people.
And here you are!
I need to make her trust me – or we are both going to die in the flames.

I'm alive, I'm still alive …
He didn't give up on me.
Oh what a nightmare!

Uff …
that was a near thing.
But hey, we made it.
Maybe she can forget what I did to her?
I'm a good cop, God knows I want to be a good cop, always there to help people. Today I could show this!

I really can't understand this.
How can anyone be so different?
This pig risked his life to save mine!!
He is a bully; he just turned into a hero. Should I forgive him?
I don't know if I can;
I have no idea what to make out of this …

Portraits of urban families

We are going to watch some more scenes of *L.A. Crash*. While watching make some notes and complete the table:

a) Summarize what happens in each scene and find a title for it.
b) Place the scene in the context of the film.
c) In how far do cinematic devices reveal more information about the family?
d) Do these family portraits match your ideas of a happy family? Why (not)?
Take into account all the other details you know about the family.

	Scene 1 (00:24:25–00:29:24)	Scene 2 (00:41:55–00:42:27)	Scene 3 (00:48:25–00:58:20)
Title			
a) Who? Where? What? Why? When?			
b) Context of the film			
c) Cinematic devices	**props:** **sound:**	**props:**	**props:**
d) Perfect family life?			

Fact box

Cinematic device	Function
• **visual symbols/props:** Which visual symbols/props are employed?	→ visual leitmotifs serve as links and help to express/ to intensify a deeper contextual meaning
• **film music/sound:** What kind of music/what (back-ground) sounds are employed?	→ to show/emphasize a mood, to create suspense, to foreshadow

Role cards for the talk show

Louise Waters

- You are Louise Waters, Graham's and Peter's mother.
- The producers of the talk show Big City Life L.A. invited you to their show with the topic "Families in focus". You agreed to take part in it and tell the true story of your family.
- At the beginning you will be asked to introduce yourself and your family situation.
- You were given some questions you could think about in preparation for the show (of course, you might be asked more questions during the show):
  - → What is an ideal family for you?
  - → In how far is your family different from this idea?
  - → What is your current situation like?
  - → What are your aims? Your dreams?
  - → What did you do to support your children?
  - → Why are Graham and Peter so different?
  - → In how far did social/outer circumstances interfere with your family affairs?
  - → What happened to your husband?
  - → Why did Peter leave you?
  - → Which choices did you make in your life that were absolutely right? Which ones would you consider as wrong choices?

Daniel Ruiz

- You are Daniel Ruiz, a locksmith. Your daughter Lara is five years old; your wife's name is Elizabeth.
- The producers of the talk show Big City Life L.A. invited you to their show with the topic "Families in focus". You agreed to take part in it and tell the true story of your family.
- At the beginning you will be asked to introduce yourself and your family situation.
- You were given some questions you could think about in preparation for the show (of course, you might be asked different questions during the show):
  - → What is an ideal family for you?
  - → In how far is your family different from this idea?
  - → What is your current situation like?
  - → What are your aims? Your dreams?
  - → What do you do to support your child? What do you want her life to be like?
  - → In how far did social/outer circumstances interfere with your family affairs?
  - → Why did you decide to move to a different neighbourhood?
  - → Which choices did you make in your life that were absolutely right? Which ones would you consider as wrong choices?

Jean Cabot

- You are Jean Cabot. You are married to the local district attorney Rick Cabot. You have a son, James.
- The producers of the talk show Big City Life L.A. invited you to their show with the topic "Families in Focus". You agreed to take part in it and tell the true story of your family.
- At the beginning you will be asked to introduce yourself and your family.
- You were given some questions you could think about in preparation for the show (of course, you might be asked different questions during the show):
  - → What is an ideal family for you?
  - → In how far is your family different from this idea?
  - → What is your current situation like?
  - → What are your aims? Your dreams?
  - → Which role does your son James play in your life?
  - → Do you love your husband? Do you think Rick cheats on you with Karen, his assistant?
  - → In how far did social/outer circumstances interfere with your family affairs?
  - → Why are you afraid of strangers?
  - → Which choices did you make in your life that were absolutely right? Which ones would you consider as wrong choices?

Component 3

Ethnic diversity and urban life as key challenges in *L.A. Crash*

In diesem *Component* geht es vorrangig darum, die Begegnungen der Charaktere genauer zu betrachten und Hintergründe und Ursachen für Verhaltensweisen zu beleuchten. Im ersten Schritt wird das Thema *Bigotry* als Überbegriff zu *stereotypes, prejudices* und *discrimination* aufgegriffen. Nachdem die Schüler bezüglich eigener Vorurteile sensibilisiert worden sind, werden entsprechende Szenen aus dem Film vertieft analysiert. Der zweite Komplex hebt die Problematik auf eine globalere Ebene, indem weitere Szenen betrachtet werden, in denen auch andere Ursachen eine gelungene Kommunikation und ein harmonisches Zusammenleben unterbinden. Warum es zu diesen Konflikten kommt und wie diese mit der Realität des Lebens in der Großstadt verknüpft sind, wird über den Filminhalt hinaus untersucht.
Zur genaueren Analyse der Szenen kann es hilfreich sein, das Drehbuch zur Verfügung zu stellen. Dieses kann unter http://www.awesomefilm.com/script/Crash.pdf heruntergeladen werden.

3.1 Being confronted with stereotypes

Die Begegnungen der verschiedenen Protagonisten im Film sind gekennzeichnet durch Intoleranz, Ablehnung und Vorurteile. Als beispielsweise Farhad im Waffengeschäft mit seiner Tochter Dorri in seiner Muttersprache Farsi spricht, assoziiert der weiße Ladenbesitzer diese mit den Terroristen des 11. September und beschimpft ihn rassistisch. Die eigentlich alltägliche Situation eskaliert aufgrund der Stereotypisierung. Die daraus entstehenden Missverständnisse, Aggressionen und Diskriminierungen lassen jeglichen Versuch erfolgreicher Kommunikation scheitern. Während der Ladenbesitzer keine Waffe an einen „Jihad-Kämpfer" verkaufen möchte, beharrt Farhad auf seinem Recht, als amerikanischer Staatsbürger eine Waffe erwerben zu dürfen. Das Aggressionspotenzial steigt auf beiden Seiten so an, dass keine erfolgreiche Kommunikation miteinander mehr stattfinden kann. Farhad muss das Geschäft verlassen.
Im Laufe des folgenden *Components* analysieren die Schüler diese und andere Szenen hinsichtlich des stereotypengeleiteten Verhaltens der Charaktere. Dazu werden die Begriffe definiert, um anschließend die Vorurteilsbildungen der Figuren im Film und deren Wirkung zu erfassen. Den Schülern soll währenddessen immer wieder eigene Voreingenommenheit bewusst gemacht werden, um mit dieser reflektierter umgehen zu können.

Im Einstieg nähern sich die Schüler dem Thema „Vorurteilsbildung" an, indem sie mit stereotypbesetzten Bildern konfrontiert werden. Ziel ist es, bei jedem Schüler bestehende klischeehafte Assoziationen zu evozieren, diese bewusst zu machen und kritisch zu hinterfragen. Die Klasse wird dazu in zwei Gruppen aufgeteilt. Die Schüler einer Gruppe erhalten jeweils das gleiche Bild von ***Copy 12*** (S. 77) sowie die dazugehörigen Fragen, ohne dass die andere Gruppe das Bild sehen kann.

Make sure that the other group cannot see your picture. Answer the questions spontaneously and make notes.

Der Austausch findet in Form eines *double circles* statt. Dazu sitzen oder stehen sich jeweils Schüler mit unterschiedlichen Bildern gegenüber.

Without showing your partner the picture, explain to him/her your reaction by answering the questions. Start with the first question.
After the signal, the outer circle moves to the left so that you have got a different partner. Then answer the second question and so on.

Nachdem sich die Schüler auf diese Weise zu ihren Bildern geäußert haben, wird der *double circle* aufgelöst und die jeweils andere Gruppe stellt im Plenum Vermutungen zur beschriebenen Figur an.

Influenced by the descriptions you received from your classmates, what kind of picture do you expect?

Anschließend dürfen die Bilder offen gelegt werden. Im Unterrichtsgespräch äußern sich die Schüler zu ihren Eindrücken und vergleichen die Reaktionen auf die beiden Bildimpulse. Folgende Fragen können das Gespräch steuern:

Are there any similarities in your reaction? Why (not)?
Why was everyone immediately able to react to the pictures?
How did personal experience influence your reaction?
Beside clothes, what else might lead to stereotypical thinking?
What are possible consequences of stereotypical thinking?
Which cases of stereotypical behaviour are depicted in *L.A. Crash*?

Die letzten Fragen implizieren Antworten, welche die Begriffe *discrimination* und *racism* beinhalten, und leiten so mit Einbezug des Filminhalts über zu einer theoretischen Betrachtung von Vorurteilen und deren Konsequenzen im sozialen Miteinander.

3.2 Stereotype – prejudice – discrimination: towards a definition

Bigotry im Kontext des Zusammenlebens von Menschen verschiedener Kulturen und Ethnizitäten bezeichnet die Tendenz, eine Person im Vergleich zu einer anderen zu bevorzugen. Es ist als Überbegriff zu *stereotype, prejudice* und *discrimination* zu sehen, welche die kognitive Ebene, affektive Ebene und die Verhaltensebene repräsentieren. Ein Mensch, welcher entsprechend seiner Vorurteile handelt, wird als *bigot* bezeichnet.

Nach der Methode *Think – Pair – Share* definieren die Schüler die vertrauten Begriffe *stereotype, prejudice, discrimination* und *racism* und halten die Ergebnisse stichwortartig fest.

How are the terms *stereotype, prejudice* and *discrimination* related?
Give definitions and illustrate them with examples. Make notes.

1. *Think* on your own.
2. *Pair* up with a partner and talk about your ideas.
3. *Share* your results with the class.

Bei leistungsstärkeren Klassen können die Kenntnisse über *bias* und *bigotry* an dieser Stelle ebenfalls abgefragt werden. Anderenfalls werden die Begriffe mithilfe von **Copy 13** (S. 78) eingeführt. Diese dient zugleich als Vergleichsmöglichkeit und Ergebnissicherung für die von den Schülern aufgestellten Definitionen.

Lösungsvorschlag zu *Copy 13* (S. 78), Teil 1:

1. bias 2. stereotype 3. prejudice 4. discrimination 5. racism 6. bigot

3.3 Bigotry in *L.A. Crash*

Der Film *L.A. Crash* lebt vom Aufeinandertreffen verschiedener Figuren mit unterschiedlichen Intentionen und Einstellungen. Die meisten Begegnungen sind durch Ablehnung und Diskriminierung gekennzeichnet. So veranlasst beispielsweise die mit Terroristen assoziierte Sprache Farhads den Waffenverkäufer zu rassistischen Äußerungen. Farhad, der sich als amerikanischer Staatsbürger sieht, wehrt sich gegen die Beschimpfungen, was die Situation eskalieren lässt. Jean Cabot, die aufgrund des Autodiebstahls durch Peter und Anthony das Vertrauen in die Gesellschaft weiter verloren hat, schließt aus dem äußeren Erscheinungsbild von Daniel auf seinen vermeintlich kriminellen Hintergrund. Diese Vorverurteilung lässt daraufhin jegliche Art verbaler Kommunikation scheitern. Daniel reagiert lediglich nonverbal auf die Beschuldigungen, indem er mit einem resignierten Blick die Schlüssel auf den Küchentisch legt. Die tragischste Begegnung findet zwischen Officer Tom Hansen und Peter statt. Hansen, der zuvor als tolerante und aufgeschlossene Person porträtiert wird, wird in dieser Szene von Stereotypen bezüglich der schwarzen Bevölkerung eingeholt. Als Peter ihm die Miniatur des Heiligen Christophorus, Schutzheiliger der Autofahrer, zeigen möchte, deutet Hansen den Griff in die Hosentasche als Griff zur Pistole und erschießt ihn in einer Kurzschlusshandlung. Cameron wird vom Filmproduzenten Fred indirekt diskriminiert, als dieser ihn auffordert, eine Szene zu wiederholen, da der schwarze Schauspieler nicht genug *slang* spricht. Um weitere Diskussionen zu vermeiden, willigt er ein.

Um Ursprünge und Folgen von Stereotypen, Vorurteilen und Diskriminierung in diesen ausgewählten Szenen zu untersuchen, finden sich die Schüler in acht Kleingruppen zusammen. Jeweils zwei Gruppen erhalten den gleichen *Screenshot* von ***Copy 13*** (S. 78) zugeteilt.

Analyze the screenshot by answering the questions on *Copy 13*. Make notes. Each group member has to be prepared to present the results.

Die Gruppenergebnisse werden nach der Methode *One stay, three stray* den Mitschülern präsentiert.

To share your results, one of you stays at your group's table to present your ideas.
The other group members find out about the other screenshots. Make sure that in the end your group has information about all four stills. Make notes while listening to the presenter.
When you hear a signal, come back to your group's table and tell your group about the other stills. Write down keywords to complete your worksheet.

Lösungsvorschlag zu *Copy 13* (S. 78), Teil 2:

Scene		
a	1.	• Farhad wants to buy a gun to protect his family and his shop. • Dorri accompanies him to translate into Farsi. • As Farhad and Dorri start to discuss about the right ammunition, the shop owner (Dirk) insults him ("Yo, Osama, plan the Jihad on your own time."). • Next scene: Daniel repairs the lock of Farhad's shop door → devastation of his shop the same night → Farhad 'shoots' Lara with the gun
	2.	• Dirk associates the foreign language with al-Qaeda, 09/11, terrorists; Farhad might use the gun for criminal acts. • Both Dirk and Farhad react aggressively. • Farhad insists on his right to buy a gun as an American citizen. • Dorri tries to calm Farhad's anger and finally buys the gun without him. • widely spread prejudices against people who speak Arabic vs. sympathy for Farhad because he absolutely has no terroristic intention and is Persian, not Arabian
b	1.	• Daniel changes the locks at the Cabots' because the keys were stolen during the carjack. • Because of Daniel's outer appearance (tattoos, short haircut, baggy trousers, 'gang member'), Jean wants the locks to be changed again in the morning. She tells Rick all this while Daniel can hear the degradation. When Daniel has finished, he leaves the keys on the kitchen table without saying a word.
	2.	• Jean judges by appearances alone and concludes that Daniel must be a criminal who sells the keys to his friends. • Daniel doesn't react impulsively to the insults but shows his emotions in his facial expression. By avoiding a conflict, Daniel acts superior to Jean who has just been a victim herself and now degrades Daniel. → sympathy for Daniel, aversion to Jean
c	1.	• Peter hitch-hikes after visiting the ice hockey game; Officer Tom Hansen stops and gives him a lift to the other side of the hill. • Their conversation escalates because Hansen reacts aggressively, apparently without any reason. In fact, he's in a bad mood because of his conflict with Officer Ryan and his superior, Lieutenant Dixon. • When Peter wants to show that, like Hansen, he also carries a miniature of St. Christopher on him, Hansen thinks he wants to get a gun out of his pocket, thus misinterpreting Peter's movement and shooting him. • When Hansen realizes his blunder, he's desperate and burns his car to destroy all evidence.
	2.	• Although Hansen actually is not a racist, in this nerve-racking situation he misinterprets the movement, led by the generalized stereotype that black people have guns (stigmatization overcomes perception). → The audience is surprised because it's the first situation in which Hansen behaves like a racist and violently. The audience is shocked by the power stereotypes might have over somebody.
d	1.	• In the Columbia Studios Cameron, the director, is shooting a TV series. • The Executive Producer (Fred) wants the scene to be taken once more because Jamal, a black boy, doesn't speak 'black enough'. • Although Cameron, as a black man, feels discriminated against himself, he agrees and orders another take.
	2.	• Jamal's way of talking doesn't fit in with Fred's image of a black boy. Therefore, he wants him to speak more according to the generalized stereotypical image. • Cameron restrains himself because he realizes Fred's set position. → Cameron is degraded. • The TV audience may have generalized stereotypes of the language of black people, which Fred wants to satisfy. → We, as the audience of *L.A. Crash*, are portrayed ourselves. → Do we have stereotypes which are met in the film to fulfil our expectations?

Im abschließenden Unterrichtsgespräch werden die Inhalte der Gruppenphase aufgegriffen und mittels Hypothesenbildung erweitert. Dazu wird darüber spekuliert, wie alternative Handlungen in den kritischen Situationen den Fortgang des Films verändert hätten.

> Can you think of alternative reactions of the characters in the scenes? What are possible consequences of these reactions for the plot? Which effect might they, in turn, have on the audience?

Mögliche Antworten:

Scene	
a	• Farhad informs about his ethnicity → Dirk might withdraw his insults → instructive for the audience but less entertaining
b	• When Daniel leaves without saying a word, Jean apologizes because she realized her overreaction and misinterpretation → the scene wouldn't maintain the tension • Rick apologizes for Jean's behavior → Jean is degraded by her husband → Jean's misbehaviour is emphasized • Daniel insults her as 'desperate housewife' → the situation escalates into an argument (soap opera style) → doesn't meet the quality of the film
c	• Hansen asks Peter what he wants to show him → Peter shows him his miniature → the scene becomes less striking because the consequences of stereotypes aren't displayed
d	• Cameron could discuss the topic with the crew and comment on the display of stereotypes → depending on how the crew reacts, either Cameron or Fred would lose → different perspectives on this topic could be presented

Um die Stundeninhalte umzuwälzen und zu vertiefen, verfassen die Schüler einen Kommentar zu folgendem Thema:

> In a film review a critic maintains: "Haggis wants to tell us that racial conflict is always bubbling beneath the surface of contemporary Los Angeles."
> Comment on this statement.
> (http://nymag.com/nymetro/movies/reviews/11872/)

3.4 Crash – more than a car accident

Wie durch den Filmtitel impliziert, passieren in *L.A. Crash* einige Autounfälle: Gleich am Anfang kollidiert das Polizeiauto von Ria und Graham mit dem der aufgebrachten Koreanerin Kim Lee. Später wird ihr Ehemann Choi von Anthony und Peter angefahren und schwerverletzt ins Krankenhaus gebracht. Und auch Christine entgeht dem Tod nur knapp, nachdem sich ihr Auto überschlagen hat und in Flammen aufzugehen droht. In der Abschlussszene wird das Motiv erneut aufgegriffen: Ein Fahrer lateinamerikanischer Herkunft fährt in Shaniquas Auto. Während es im Folgenden zunächst um die wörtliche Konnotation des Begriffs „crash" geht, liegt der Schwerpunkt der weiteren Analyse auf der metaphorischen Bedeutung im Sinne der zwischenmenschlichen Kollisionen.

Als Einstieg präsentiert der Lehrer die Definition des Wortes „crash" auf Folie. Die Schüler äußern sich spontan im Unterrichtsgespräch, indem sie den gesuchten Begriff nennen und Beispiele aus dem Film aufzählen.

Read the definition. Which term is described? Find examples from the film that illustrate the definition.

(noun): Accident in which a vehicle hits something, for example another vehicle, usually causing damage and often injuring or killing the passengers.

Oxford Advanced Learner's Dictionary (2005)

Mögliche Antworten:

- Ria's car crash with Kim Lee's car in the first scene
- Christine's overturned car
- Choi is run over by Anthony and Peter
- Shaniqua's rear-end collision at the very end of the film

Neben diesen tatsächlichen Autounfällen kommt es aus unterschiedlichen Gründen auch zu zahlreichen zwischenmenschlichen Kollisionen. Der Titel *Crash* hat im Film eine überwiegend metaphorische Bedeutung. Die meisten Begegnungen sind von einem aggressiven Ton geprägt. Die Kommunikation zwischen den Menschen und somit auch ein friedliches, tolerantes Miteinander scheitern aus den verschiedensten Gründen. Fast jede Begegnung eskaliert in einer mehr oder weniger drastischen Weise.

Zu Beginn des Films überfallen Anthony und Peter die wohlhabenden Cabots und rauben deren Auto. Vorausgegangen ist dieser Tat eine eindeutige Geste von Jean, die nachts auf der Straße aus Angst vor den beiden dunkelhäutigen Männern Ricks Arm greift und so indirekt ihre Skepsis ausdrückt. Anthony und Peter wiederum fühlen sich von Jeans Gestik angegriffen, weshalb sie umgehend die von Stereotypen geleiteten Erwartungen bestätigen. Der bewaffnete Überfall, bei dem auch die Hausschlüssel gestohlen wurden, löst einen Streit zwischen den Cabots aus. Jean, die dem Schlosser Daniel aufgrund seines äußeren Erscheinungsbildes nicht traut, verlangt von Rick, die Schlösser am nächsten Morgen erneut tauschen zu lassen. Als dieser ihre Ängste nicht ernst nimmt, verschärft sich der Ton zwischen den Eheleuten.
Als der um seinen Vater besorgte Officer Ryan bei der *Health Maintenance Organisation* anruft, eskaliert das Gespräch, da Shaniqua ihm keine unmittelbare Hilfe anbieten kann. Auch das Gespräch in Shaniquas Büro am nächsten Tag scheitert an den von Stereotypen und negativen Vorerfahrungen geprägten Grundhaltungen der beiden. Shaniqua lässt John Ryan vom Sicherheitsdienst aus ihrem Büro werfen.
Als Farhad seinen verwüsteten Laden vorfindet, vermutet er Daniel hinter der Tat, da dieser am Abend zuvor das Türschloss zwar ausgewechselt, ihm aber zugleich geraten hat, die Tür zeitnah ganz auszutauschen. Um sich zu rächen, fährt er zu Daniel und bedroht ihn und seine Tochter mit der neu erworbenen Waffe, nicht wissend, dass diese lediglich Platzpatronen enthält. Nur diesem Zufall ist es zu verdanken, dass Farhad nicht zum Mörder der kleinen Lara, Daniels Tochter, wird.
Ganz anders verläuft dagegen die Begegnung zwischen dem Polizisten Tom Hansen und Peter. Als Officer Hansen Peters Griff in die Hosentasche als Griff zur Waffe fehlinterpretiert, geschieht das Unglück: Er erschießt Peter, der ihm eigentlich nur seine Heiligenfigur zeigen wollte. An dieser Stelle erreicht der Film seinen dramatischen Höhepunkt.

Um auf die Doppeldeutigkeit des Filmtitels hinzuführen, passen die Schüler die gegebene Definition der metaphorischen Bedeutung von *Crash* an.

Beside car accidents, there are other situations in the film in which people collide with each other.
With a partner, reformulate the given definition so that it applies to this metaphorical use of "crash".

Some of you are asked to write the definition on transparency snippets to present in front of the class.

Mögliche Antwort:

Definition of crash as a metaphor in the film:
encounter in which a person meets another person, usually causing damage and often hurting, injuring or killing the other one (for different reasons)

Auf der Grundlage der vorgestellten Definitionen einigt sich die Klasse auf eine gemeinsame Formulierung, welche in der Tafelmitte festgehalten wird. Das Tafelbild wird im weiteren Stundenverlauf von den Schülern erweitert.

In groups, find various examples of interpersonal conflicts from the film. Agree on three significant interpersonal crashes and write them on the paper slips.

Als Ergebnissicherung wird das begonnene Tafelbild durch die Beispiele der Schüler erweitert, die sie auf Papierstreifen notieren und an der Tafel anbringen.

Place your paper slips on the board and briefly explain the context. Only add new examples to avoid doublings.

Die zwischenmenschlichen Konflikte werden im Film offensichtlich und teils sehr drastisch dargestellt. Die Auslöser und Hintergründe müssen aber überwiegend vom Zuschauer puzzleartig zusammengesetzt und genauer beleuchtet werden. Geleitet von ***Copy 14*** (S. 79) wird dieser Schritt von den Schülern nach der Methode *Think – Pair – Share* vollzogen.

Describe what happens when the characters meet and give possible reasons for the conflicts. Which social/ethnic/political ... circumstances lead to the interpersonal crashes?

Nach dem Abgleich mit einem Partner erfolgt der Austausch im Plenum, welcher mit folgender Frage abgeschlossen werden kann:

Movies don't always depict reality accurately. Which of these problems do you think really exist in L.A.?

Texte über landeskundliches Hintergrundwissen (***Copies 16–18,*** S. 83 ff.) sollen es ermöglichen, die Frage fundiert beantworten zu können. Dazu bekommt jeder Schüler das Übersichtsblatt ***Copy 15*** (S. 81) sowie eine der drei Quellen zugeordnet, auf deren Grundlage er einen *2-minute talk* erarbeitet. Diese Methode bereitet die Schüler auf die Kommunikationsprüfung vor, in deren Verlauf ebenfalls ein Kurzvortrag erfolgt.

Reality check: In how far does the film *L.A. Crash* give us an authentic picture of urban challenges in Los Angeles? Read the text/interpret the statistics and think about scenes from the film which are related to this topic. Prepare a 2-minute talk.

Die Informationsweitergabe an die Mitschüler erfolgt in Form eines Gruppenmosaiks, wobei die Schüler so lange anderen Mitschülern begegnen, bis sie zu jedem Thema mindestens einen Vortrag gehört und die wichtigsten Punkte auf ***Copy 15*** (S. 81) notiert haben.

Die in der Stunde sowohl auf der Grundlage des Films als auch auf landeskundlicher Ebene erarbeiteten Ergebnisse werden in einem Schreibauftrag zusammengefasst und weiterentwickelt.

Society is to be blamed for individual failure. Discuss on the basis of the film *L.A. Crash*. (200 – 300 words)

Die Schülerprodukte werden in der nächsten Stunde durch eine *peer conference* gewürdigt: Die Mitschüler lesen Texte unterschiedlicher Autoren durch, um schwerwiegende Fehler zu korrigieren und Positives hervorzuheben.

Let me introduce ...

- What kind of emotions instantly come to you when you see this picture?
- Who taught you about this individual?
- What did they teach you?
- How has the media (TV, movies, books, stories) shaped your image of this individual?

adapted from http://www.tolerance.org/activity/clothing-based-bias [04.07.2013]

Let me introduce ...

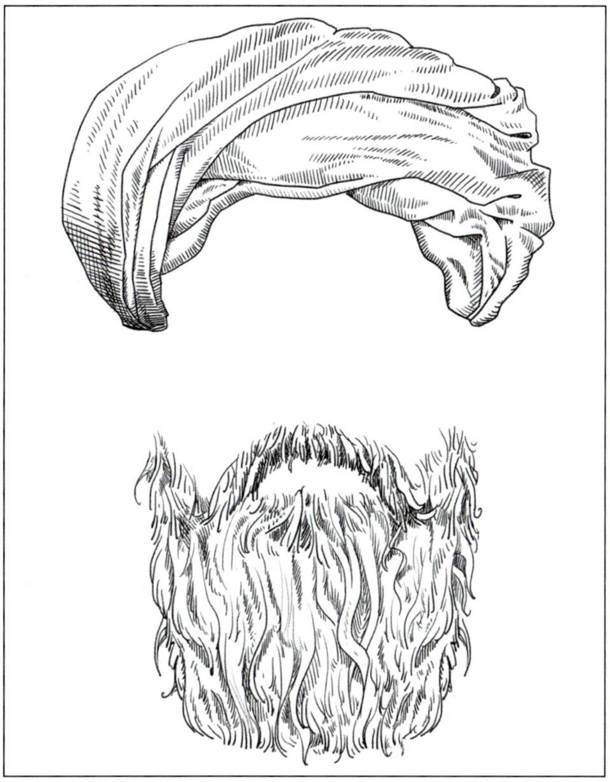

- What kind of emotions instantly come to you when you see this picture?
- Who taught you about this individual?
- What did they teach you?
- How has the media (TV, movies, books, stories) shaped your image of this individual?

adapted from http://www.tolerance.org/activity/clothing-based-bias [04.07.2013]

Bigotry

1. Match the terms with the definitions.

stereotype – racism – bigot
prejudice – bias – discrimination

1.		tendency to prefer one person or thing to another, and to favour that person or thing
2.		fixed general image or set of characteristics that a lot of people believe represent a particular type of person or thing; cognitive bias; strongly influenced by culture and society
3.		unreasonable dislike of a particular group of people or things, or a preference for one group of people or things over another; affective bias
4.		practice of treating one person or group of people less fairly or less well than other people or groups; behavioural component of bias
5.		belief that people of some races are inferior to others, and the behaviour which is the result of this belief
6.		someone who has strong, unreasonable prejudices or opinions and will not change them, even when they are proved to be wrong

2. Describe the situation in the screenshot. What has happened to the characters before? What happens after?

3. Which stereotypes and prejudices can you identify? Who is the bigot in this situation? How do the characters respond? Why? What kind of reaction is this supposed to evoke in the audience?

a

b

c

d

Crash

1. **What happens when the following characters meet? Describe the situations briefly.**

Shaniqua and John Ryan
reasons:

Daniel and Farhad
reasons:

Anthony + Peter and Rick + Jean
reasons:

Crash

Peter and Tom Hansen
reasons:

Rick and Jean
reasons:

2. **What are the reasons for the conflicts?**
   The following expressions might help you to describe the triggers.

failure of institutions *mistrust* *alienation* *racism* *stereotypes* *clash of different ethnicities* *social differences* *lack of social bonding* *misinterpretation* *frustration*

Crash (possible solution)

1. What happens when the following characters meet? Describe the situations briefly.

Shaniqua and John Ryan
Officer John Ryan calls the HMO to seek help for his ill father. Shaniqua cannot help him. This is why he insults her.
reasons: failure of institutions, racism, frustration

Daniel and Farhad
Farhad doesn't trust Daniel when he advises him to replace the door. The situation escalates. The next morning Farhad finds his shop looted. As the insurance doesn't cover the damage, he decides to take revenge by shooting Daniel.
reasons: mistrust, clash of different ethnicities, frustration

Anthony + Peter and Rick + Jean
When Jean passes by, her body language expresses the fear Anthony and Peter evoke in her. Driven by this reaction, they confirm the stereotype by stealing their car.
reasons: racism, stereotypes, clash of different ethnicities, social differences

Crash

encounter in which a person meets another person, usually causing damage and often hurting, injuring or killing the other one (for different reasons)

Peter and Tom Hansen
Peter hitch-hikes. Hansen gives him a lift. When Peter reaches into his pocket to show him the statuette of St. Christopher, Hansen thinks he wants to pull out his gun and shoots him.
reasons: mistrust, stereotypes, misinterpretation

Rick and Jean
They have an argument about changing the locks again. Jean doesn't feel to be taken seriously. After her accident, when she needs comfort, neither he nor her best friend are there to help her. Only the Latin American housekeeper, Maria, is there to console her.
reasons: alienation, lack of social bonding, frustration

2. What are the reasons for the conflicts?
The following expressions might help you to describe the triggers.

failure of institutions *mistrust* *alienation* *racism* *stereotypes* *clash of different ethnicities*
social differences *lack of social bonding* *misinterpretation* *frustration*

Urban challenges – reality check

Read your text and write down the most important facts in the corresponding column.
With the help of your notes, prepare a 2-minute talk about the topic and illustrate it with examples from the film.
Meet experts who read the other texts. While listening to their informative talks, complete the table.

Source:	Copy 16: Americans and their guns: To ban or not to ban?	Copy 17: Healthcare in the US: HMO Insurance Plans	Copy 18: Multiethnic L.A.: Demography of the city of Los Angeles
Important facts:			
Scenes from the film *L.A. Crash* dealing with this topic:			

Urban challenges – reality check (possible solution)

Read your text and write down the most important facts in the corresponding column.
With the help of your notes, prepare a 2-minute talk about the topic and illustrate it with examples from the film.
Meet experts who read the other texts. While listening to their informative talks, complete the table.

Source:	Copy 16: Americans and their guns: To ban or not to ban?	Copy 17: Healthcare in the US: HMO Insurance Plans	Copy 18: Multiethnic L.A.: Demography of the city of Los Angeles
Important facts:	• 58% of Americans favour a ban on assault weapons. • However, a new law was squelched because of political reasons. • Alternatives for the ban on assault weapons: expanding the criminal background check system, destroy the structure of arms trade. • The National Rifle Association (NRA) is very powerful in the US (e.g. they rate congressional candidates). • To purchase and possess guns is enshrined in the US tradition (cf. Second Amendment to the United States Constitution).	• HMO = Health Maintenance Organization, network of providers of healthcare services • In case of illness you first have to contact your PCP (primary care physician) who may refer you to a specialist. • There usually is no coverage for out-of-network services. • The latest HMO report shows that there is a lack of proper treatment of adults with chronic medical conditions. • It is not easy to get the recommended care for people with chronic conditions.	• Los Angeles is the second-biggest city in the US. • Like in all other cities ranked, there is an increase of population. • Compared to New York (biggest city) and Chicago (third-biggest city), Los Angeles has a very low population density. • Los Angeles is the most culturally diverse city in the US. • L.A. has the largest number of people of Hispanic and Latino origins of any urban city in the US (44.4% of the population of L.A.). • L.A. maintains the second largest Asian population in the US (14.5% of the population of L.A.). • white population: 31.6% • black population: 6.7 % • 57% of the families living in L.A. don't speak English at home.
Scenes from the film *L.A. Crash* dealing with this topic:	• Farhad in the gun shop • Farhad shooting Daniel/Lara • Peter and Anthony carjacking Rick and Jean	• Ryan consulting Shaniqua in order to achieve a better treatment of his father's urinary infection	• diversity of ethnicities portrayed in the film (e.g. Daniel is Hispanic, Kim Lee and Choi are Korean) • Farhad and Dorri talk to each other in Farsi

Gun crime

Los Angeles Times

Americans and their guns: A majority supports an assault weapons ban. But our history and culture get in the way.

March 21, 2013, Los Angeles Times Editorial Board

The 58% of Americans who favor a ban on assault weapons got a sad lesson in Washington politics this week when a major bill to end their sale, and to eliminate the high-capacity magazines that allow mass killers to do their awful work without pausing to reload, was effectively squelched.

squelched suppressed

The reason? After Sen. Dianne Feinstein (D-Calif.) drafted an improved version of her former assault weapons ban, [...] Senate Majority Leader Harry Reid (D-Nev.) stripped it out of a broader gun control package. Reid calculated that Feinstein's measure would attract only about 40 votes, not enough to overcome a filibuster; he wants to focus instead on restrictions with more bipartisan support, such as expanding the criminal background check system and cracking down on straw purchasers who buy guns on behalf of criminals.

to strip out to remove from

filibuster parliamentary procedure to delay a vote on a given proposal

But something seems wrong with the math here. If such a large proportion of Americans favors a weapons ban [...] – why the dearth of congressional support? Feinstein is pretty sure she has the answer. "You'd think the Congress would listen, but they clearly listen to the National Rifle Assn.," she complained.

dearth of *Mangel an*

She has a point. The NRA exercises its influence in many ways, starting with its ratings of congressional candidates – anything less than an A grade from the organization could turn off a powerful voting bloc. Then there is its legendary fundraising prowess; it spent $18.6 million during the 2012 election cycle, according to the Sunlight Foundation. Yet this is an organization with somewhere between 3 million and 4.5 million members (exact numbers are hard to come by), in a country where 70 million say they own guns, and millions more support broad gun rights. There is something else in the American character that makes us love our guns.

prowess ability

Some people love to hunt and some legitimately feel the need for self-protection, but our obsession with overpowered weapons runs deeper than the working-class frustration and bitterness that cause us to "cling to guns and religion," as President Obama notoriously said during a campaign speech in 2008. For some, it stems from the feelings of power one gets by carrying a massive firearm; for others, it's a distrust of the government's ability to protect us, or paranoid fantasies fueled by exaggerated TV news coverage of crime, not to mention violent video games, movies and so on. Certainly part of it is rooted in our history, in which freedom had to be won by the people by force of arms, leading to a constitutional amendment to keep firearms available. At its base is a simple but powerful emotion: fear. [...]

to stem from to derive from

Healthcare services

HMO Insurance Plans

What is an HMO plan?

HMO means "Health Maintenance Organization". HMO plans offer a wide range of healthcare services through a network of providers who agree to supply services to members. With an HMO you'll likely have coverage for a broader range of preventive healthcare services than you would through another type of plan.

How does an HMO plan work?

As a member of an HMO, you'll be required to choose a primary care physician (PCP). Your PCP will take care of most of your healthcare needs. Before you can see a specialist, you'll need to obtain a referral from your PCP. Though there are many variations, HMO plans typically to enable members to have lower out-of-pocket healthcare expenses. You may not be required to pay a deductible before coverage starts and your co-payments will likely be minimal. You also typically won't have to submit any of your own claims to the insurance company. However, keep in mind that you'll likely have no coverage for services rendered by out-of-network providers or for services rendered without a proper referral from your PCP.

http://www.ehealthinsurance.com/health-plans/hmo/ [04.07.2013]

to be required to do sth. it is necessary to do sth.
referral document which confirms the recommendation to consult a specialist
deductible certain amount of money that the policy holder has to pay for every treatment

Los Angeles Times

California issues annual ratings for health plans, physician groups

March 27, 2013, By Chad Terhune

Kaiser Permanente was the only HMO to earn a top four-star rating for providing recommended care on California's annual report card, while Cigna and United Healthcare led the way with three-star ratings among PPO plans. The report issued Wednesday on California's biggest HMOs and other health insurance plans showed improvement in care for children, but mixed results for treating adults with chronic medical conditions. [...]

State officials said health insurers and physicians are making strides in giving children their immunizations, checking them for excess body fat and avoiding the overuse of antibiotics for throat infections. But the quality of treatment for patients suffering from diabetes, heart disease and other chronic conditions varied widely among insurers and physician groups, according to the state.

to make strides to make good progress

Many HMO patients expressed frustration at "[not] getting care easily." On that measure, seven HMOs including Kaiser's Southern California system were rated poor, or just one star. [...] In the Los Angeles area, the medical groups of UCLA, Cedars-Sinai and HealthCare Partners all received three out of four stars on providing the recommended care.

Multiethnic L.A.

Cities ranked by population as of July 1, 2012

Rank	City	State	2012 Estimate	2010 Census	Change	2010 Population density
1	New York	New York	8,336,697	8,175,133	+1.98%	27,012 per sq mi
2	**Los Angeles**	**California**	**3,857,799**	**3,792,621**	**+1.72%**	**8,092 per sq mi**
3	Chicago	Illinois	2,714,856	2,695,598	+0.71%	11,842 per sq mi
4	Houston	Texas	2,160,821	2,100,263	+2.88%	3,501 per sq mi
5	Philadelphia	Pennsylvania	1,547,607	1,526,006	+1.42%	11,379 per sq mi

sq mi = square mile, 1 mile = 1609,344 meter

Data: United States Census Bureau

Demography of the city of Los Angeles

[Los Angeles] is the most culturally diverse city in the United States [...]. With more than 5.7 million people, the Los Angeles Metropolitan Area has the largest number of people of Hispanic and Latino origins of any metro area in the United States. While the Mexican population makes up 44.4% (4.36 million) of L.A.'s total population (12.8 million), establishing it as the largest racial/ethnic group in the city, L.A.'s Hispanic/Latino population is very diverse: Salvadoran (381,519), Guatemalan (231,304), Puerto Rican (55,699), and Cuban (49,702), Honduran (46,044), and Nicaraguan (40,607). Moreover, the L.A. Metro Area [...] maintains the second largest Asian population (14.5% of L.A.'s total pop.) in the United States, consisting of significant Chinese (416,042), Filipino (393,170), Korean (304,198), Vietnamese (271,234), and Japanese (134,563) populations. Additionally, the "City of Angels" also contains significant White and Black populations, the former estimated at 31.6% and the latter accounting for 6.7% of L.A. Metro's total population.

Duke University, http://sites.duke.edu/thenetworkfordfoundationgrant/demographics-of-4-cities/ [04.07.2013]

Language spoken at home, City of Los Angeles (2011)

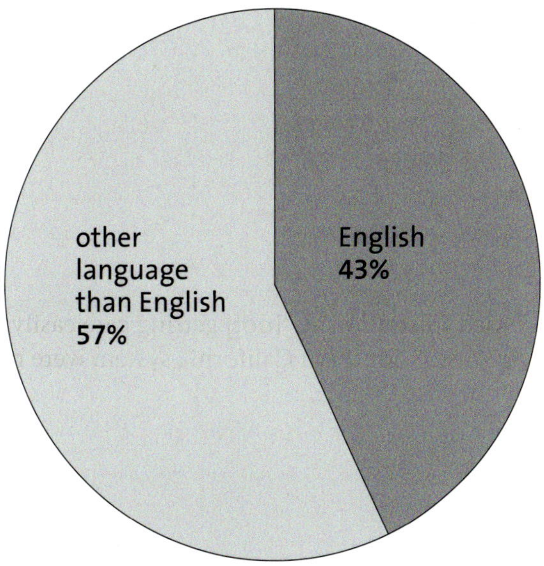

Data: United States Census Bureau

Component 4

What is *L.A. Crash* about? – Wrapping it up

Für den abschließenden *Component* wurde ein produktorientierter Ansatz gewählt. Zunächst analysieren die Schüler im Sinne der Medienkompetenz *(media literacy)* die Eigenschaften und Funktionen von Filmtrailern, um dann die daraus gewonnenen Erkenntnisse kreativ umzusetzen. Unter Einbezug des Filmwissens entsteht in Gruppenarbeit ein Entwurf für einen Trailer zu *L.A. Crash.* Auf diese Weise werden die thematisch-interpretatorischen Ergebnisse noch einmal reflektiert und die Unterrichtseinheit wird durch Rückbezug auf die anfängliche Arbeit mit dem DVD-Cover und den Zitaten abgerundet.

Als Einstieg in das abschließende Unterrichtsmodul wird ein Rückbezug zur ersten Stunde hergestellt. Dazu wird die Folie mit der Mindmap mit den Hypothesen zu Filminhalten und Charakteren aufgelegt.

> Here are your speculations about the film which we collected in the very first lesson.
>
> Which of your hypotheses can be verified now that we know the whole film?
> Which ideas didn't turn out to be true and why not?
> Which other topics does the film show that we should add to our mind map?

In einem Unterrichtsgespräch gleichen die Schüler ihre Vermutungen, die sie vor dem Sehen des Films anhand von Zitaten und dem DVD-Cover geäußert haben, mit ihren jetzigen Kenntnissen ab. Vor allem thematisch wird es einige Übereinstimmungen geben; neu gewonnene Kenntnisse können ergänzt werden. So wird sich bestätigen, dass der Film *L.A. Crash* das Leben im Großstadtdschungel nachzeichnet und Probleme beleuchtet, die bei den zufälligen Begegnungen verschiedener Menschen mit unterschiedlichen soziokulturellen Hintergründen entstehen. Die anfängliche Mindmap wird auf diese Weise also nach und nach modifiziert und es entsteht eine Sammlung der wichtigsten Aspekte, die während der Unterrichtseinheit beobachtet und behandelt wurden.

Lösungsvorschlag:

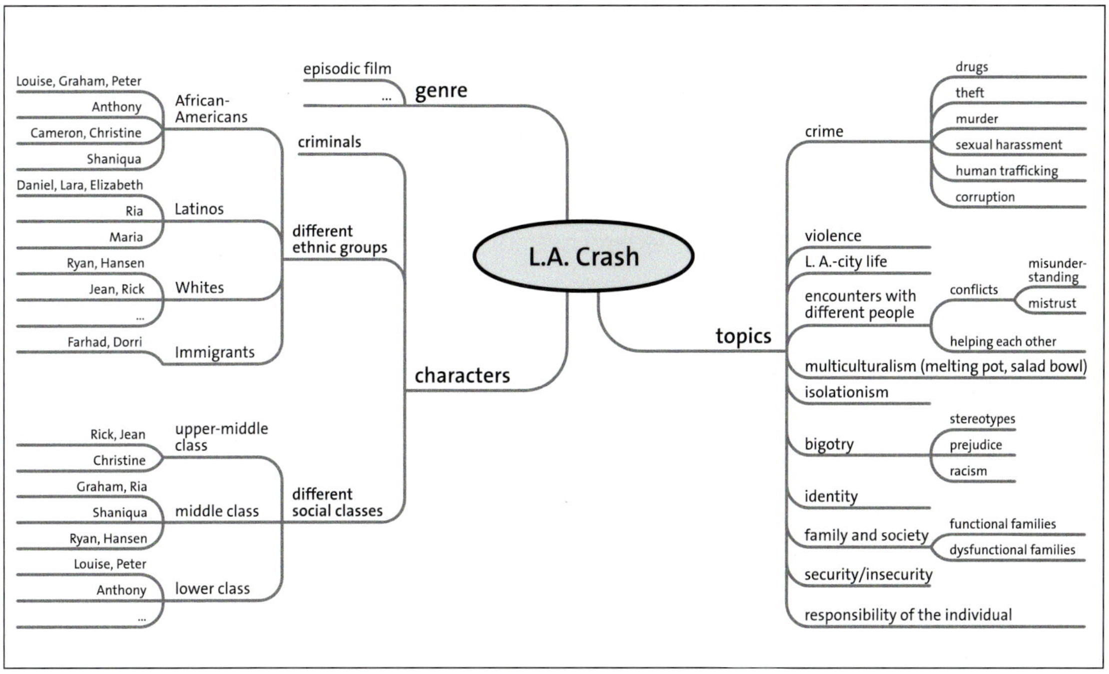

4.1 Characteristics and functions of trailers

Im folgenden Unterrichtsschritt werden Kennzeichen und Funktionen von Filmtrailern als Werbemittel erarbeitet. Als Analysebeispiel wird den Schülern dazu der Trailer des 2009 erschienenen Films *Crossing Over* präsentiert, der unter folgendem Link zu finden ist: http://www.youtube.com/watch?v=a1kqcuDKqr8 (letzter Zugriff: August 2013). Natürlich wäre das Zeigen anderer Filmtrailer auch denkbar, allerdings ist *Crossing Over* dem Film *L.A. Crash* in struktureller und thematischer Hinsicht ähnlich, sodass ein zu starkes Abweichen vom thematischen Kontext vermieden werden kann. Die Schüler notieren aufgrund ihrer Beobachtungen typische Merkmale eines Filmtrailers auf zuvor ausgeteilte Metaplankarten. Der Trailer sollte dazu mindestens zwei Mal abgespielt werden.

> We are going to watch the trailer of the film *Crossing Over*.
> Examine the characteristic features of a trailer. While watching, make notes.
> Use an extra snippet for each idea.

Im nächsten Schritt machen sich die Schüler Gedanken und Notizen zu den Funktionen eines Trailers. Dazu können Karten in einer anderen Farbe oder Form ausgehändigt werden:

> What are the functions of a trailer? Again, use the snippets to write down your ideas.

Die Ergebnisse der Schüler werden als Metaplan festgehalten, sodass sie anschaulich auf einer Pinnwand oder an der Tafel kategorisiert werden können. Ein oder zwei Schüler übernehmen die Moderation der Ideensammlung. Alternativ können die Ideen auch auf Folie oder an der Tafel gesammelt werden.

Mögliche Lösungen:

Characteristics of trailers

- viewing restrictions are shown at the beginning on a green screen (**rating card**)
- **short** (about 2 minutes and 30 seconds long)
- **selected scenes** that reveal something but not too much about the film's content/plot/mood/atmosphere/protagonists/...
- **short shots** and **quick cuts** of some of the most exciting/spectacular situations of the film (= key scenes)
- only short **snippets of dialogues** between characters are shown, not whole conversations
- the cuts are not necessarily in the same chronological order as in the film
- **cliffhangers** (open endings of different plotlines)
- establish the genre, the key themes, the actors and the director
- catchy **music** and **sound effects**
- **voiceover** that gives more information/asks key questions
- **intertitles** with key questions/quotes
- **on-screen texts** (names of the actors, the director, quotes, ...)
- the **title** of the film is shown towards the end/several times
- ...

Functions of trailers

- make people go to the movies/buy the DVD/...
- attract a certain target group
- cause curiosity about the plot
- inform about key themes and genre
- introduce the stars (most famous actors of the cast)
- touch emotionally
- manipulate
- ...

4.2 Designing a trailer for *L.A. Crash*

Für die anschließende Unterrichtsphase wird die Klasse in Kleingruppen eingeteilt. In diesen Gruppen wird ein Vorschlag für einen Trailer erarbeitet, indem ein *storyboard* gezeichnet und ein dazugehöriges *script* geschrieben wird (***Copy 19***, S. 90). Auch an dieser Stelle kann das *fact sheet „Film/movie terminology"* (***Copy 6***, S. 61) wieder eingesetzt werden. Die Schüler bestimmen die wichtigsten Szenen, Zitate und Themen des Films und erarbeiten ein Konzept für eine überzeugende Präsentation des Trailers. Dabei wenden sie die neu gewonnenen Erkenntnisse zu Merkmalen und Funktionen von Filmtrailern direkt praktisch an, wälzen aber auch noch einmal Inhalte und Ergebnisse der vorangegangenen Unterrichtsstunden um.

Für die Gruppenarbeitsphase gibt der Lehrer folgenden Arbeitsauftrag:

> Paul Haggis, the director of *L.A. Crash*, asked several post-production companies to work out a proposal for the trailer of his film. Imagine, you are one of those companies and you want to be awarded the contract. In your team, design a trailer and create a storyboard that illustrates your ideas – but before you start, decide on a name for your company. One member of your team will present your draft.

Es bietet sich an, für diese Aufgabe das Arbeitsblatt (***Copy 19***, S. 90) auf ein größeres Format (DIN A3) zu kopieren, damit die Ergebnisse besser vor der Klasse visualisiert und präsentiert werden können.

4.3 Presenting the trailer

Es wird ein Repräsentant bestimmt, der das Ergebnis möglichst werbewirksam vorstellt (***Copy 20***, S. 91). Gemeinsam mit seiner Gruppe erarbeitet dieser zunächst eine einminütige Präsentation, mit der er Paul Haggis und sein Team (also den Lehrer und die Klassenkameraden) vom Trailervorschlag seiner *production company* überzeugen möchte. Dazu erhalten die Repräsentanten den schriftlichen Arbeitsauftrag von ***Copy 20*** (S. 91), den sie dann in ihrer jeweiligen Gruppe kommunizieren. Für die Anmoderation der Präsentationsphase gibt sich der Lehrer als Paul Haggis aus, die Klasse ist „sein Team“:

> I invited you today to convince my team and me of your idea for the trailer of our new film *L.A. Crash*. The best proposal will be chosen for our advertising campaign.

Nachdem alle Repräsentanten das Konzept mündlich vorgestellt haben, werden die Poster an der Wand entlang aufgehängt, sodass sich alle Schüler bei einem *Gallery Walk* nochmals ein genaueres Bild von den Produkten ihrer Mitstreiter machen können. Jeder Schüler hat dann die Möglichkeit, für eine Idee – die nicht die seiner eigenen Gruppe sein sollte – zu votieren. Die Schüler kleben dazu kleine Punktesticker unter die Plakate. Die Gruppe, deren Vorschlag die meisten Punkte sammelt, erhält den Zuschlag des Regisseurs. Einzelne Schüler begründen im Plenum ihre Wahl.

> You now have the chance to take a closer look at the storyboards and the scripts. Choose the best proposal and mark it with the sticker. Be prepared to give reasons for your choice. It goes without saying that you can't vote for your own group's proposal.

Wenn es die Zeit erlaubt, kann der Klasse zum Abschluss noch der Originaltrailer von *L.A. Crash* präsentiert werden. Die Schüler vergleichen ihn mit den Vorschlägen der Gruppen und äußern im Unterrichtsgespräch ihre Meinung.

> Let's compare your results with the original trailer for *L.A. Crash*.
> Do you think the post-production company did a good job? Why (not)?

A trailer for *L.A. Crash*

On the basis of what you found out about features and functions of a film trailer, design a trailer for ***L.A. Crash*****:**

Draw a storyboard and write a script for the trailer.

Decide on topics, key scenes, key quotes, intertitles, voiceover, music, etc.

Each member of your group has to be prepared to present your proposal in front of the class.

Representing the production company

- You were chosen to present your company's proposal for the *L.A. Crash* trailer.
- With your group, decide on the strong points of your trailer.
- Prepare a **one-minute talk** in which you introduce your company and convince Paul Haggis and his team that your trailer is the best for advertising *L.A. Crash.*
- Practise your talk in your group, timing yourself.

Here are some phrases that might be of some help:
- There is no doubt that …
- If you choose our proposal …
- We are convinced that …
- What makes our trailer the best for your film is …
- People will flock into the cinemas to see your film because …

Representing the production company

- You were chosen to present your company's proposal for the *L.A. Crash* trailer.
- With your group, decide on the strong points of your trailer.
- Prepare a **one-minute talk** in which you introduce your company and convince Paul Haggis and his team that your trailer is the best for advertising *L.A. Crash.*
- Practise your talk in your group, timing yourself.

Here are some phrases that might be of some help:
- There is no doubt that …
- If you choose our proposal …
- We are convinced that …
- What makes our trailer the best for your film is …
- People will flock into the cinemas to see your film because …

Representing the production company

- You were chosen to present your company's proposal for the *L.A. Crash* trailer.
- With your group, decide on the strong points of your trailer.
- Prepare a **one-minute talk** in which you introduce your company and convince Paul Haggis and his team that your trailer is the best for advertising *L.A. Crash.*
- Practise your talk in your group, timing yourself.

Here are some phrases that might be of some help:
- There is no doubt that …
- If you choose our proposal …
- We are convinced that …
- What makes our trailer the best for your film is …
- People will flock into the cinemas to see your film because …

Bildnachweis

S. 3: © 2005 Lions Gate Entertainment; S. 6 (von o. nach u.): Richard Goldschmidt, David Shankbone, http://www.yomiperry.com, © picture-alliance/AP Photo; S. 7 (von o. nach u.): Vanessa Lua, Photo by Michael Buckner/WireImage, www.listal.com, lukeford.net, Mingle MediaTV, Foto: Bauer Griffin, US Department of Labor, CineMagia.ro; S. 8 (von o. nach u.): © Chris Pizzello/Invision/AP, File, David Shankbone, David Shankbone, Brad Bethell, © 2012 Larry D. Moore, gdcgraphics, ministryofstories; S. 9 (von o. nach u.): © Jason Merritt/Getty Images, © Alberto E. Rodriguez/Getty Images, © kino-teatr.ru; S. 25, 33, 34, 41, 48, 64 u., 65, 66, 78: © 2004 ApolloProScreen GmbH & Co. Filmproduktion KG; S. 61: Reinhild Kassing/Verlagsarchiv Schöningh; S. 64 o.: U.S. Navy; S. 77: Matthias Berghahn/Verlagsarchiv Schöningh

Sollte trotz aller Bemühungen um korrekte Urheberangaben ein Irrtum unterlaufen sein, bitten wir darum, sich mit dem Verlag in Verbindung zu setzen, damit wir eventuell erforderliche Korrekturen vornehmen können.

Materialien zum Schwerpunktthema
„Challenges and Choices in an Insecure World (Focus USA)“

Challenges and Choices in an Insecure World (Focus USA), das **neue Schwerpunktthema im Englisch-Abitur** in Baden-Württemberg, beleuchtet zentrale Aspekte der soziokulturellen, politischen und historischen Dimensionen unserer modernen Welt mit dem Schwerpunkt USA. Die sukzessive Erarbeitung dieses anspruchsvollen Themas wird über ein mehrteiliges Materialienangebot gewährleistet:

Balancing Freedom and Safety
Von Ulrike Klein und Gabriele Kugler-Euerle

Themenheft
164 S., vierfarb.
zahlr. Abb., kart.
Best.-Nr. **040 190**

Lehrerhandreichung
ca. 200 S., DIN A4
mit Audio-CD, kart.
Best.-Nr. **040 191**

L.A. Crash

Unterrichtsmodell
Von Annika Heider
und Iris Onderka
93 S., DIN A4, kart.
Best.-Nr. **041 168**

Interpretationshilfe
Von Ulrike Klein und
Gabriele Kugler-Euerle
ca. 96 S., einige Abb., kart.
Best.-Nr. **041 161**

Close-Up: Interaktive Filmanalyse L.A. Crash
CD-ROM
Best.-Nr. **062 486**

Jeannette Walls: Half Broke Horses
A True-Life Novel
Von Ulrike Klein und Gabriele Kugler-Euerle

Textausgabe
215 S., einige Abb., kart.
Best.-Nr. **041 164**

Unterrichtsmodell
128 S., DIN A4, kart.
Best.-Nr. **041 169**

Interpretationshilfe
ca. 96 S., einige Abb., kart.
Best.-Nr. **041 162**

Fordern Sie unseren Prospekt zur kompletten Reihe an:
Informationen 0800 / 18 18 787 (freecall)
info@schoeningh-schulbuch.de / www.schoeningh-schulbuch.de

Schöningh

Schöningh Verlag • Postfach 2540 • 33055 Paderborn

EinFach Englisch
Unterrichtsmodelle

Herausgegeben von Hans Kröger in Zusammenarbeit mit Carmen Mendez

Ausgewählte Titel der Reihe:

Cultures in Conflict?
Literature on Ethnic Relationships
115 S., DIN A4, kart. Best.-Nr. 041220
Audio-CD: 74 Min. Best.-Nr. 062407
Textausgabe: 148 S. Best.-Nr. 041218

Echoes of the Empire.
The Mixed Voices of a Colonial Past
20th Century English Short Stories
119 S., DIN A4, kart. Best.-Nr. 041223
Audio-CD: 78 Min. Best.-Nr. 062405
Textausgabe: 168 S. Best.-Nr. 041224

Political Speeches
Historical & Topical Issues
127 S., DIN A4, kart. Best.-Nr. 041236
Audio-CD: 70 Min. Best.-Nr. 062409
Textausgabe: 132 S. Best.-Nr. 041234

Utopia and Dystopia
Exploring Alternative Worlds
92 S., DIN A4, kart. Best.-Nr. 041204
Textausgabe: 92 S. Best.-Nr. 041202

Bend it Like Beckham
Filmanalyse
86 S., DIN A4, geh. Best.-Nr. 041212

Dead Poets Society
Filmanalyse
67 S., DIN A4, geh. Best.-Nr. 041255

East is East
Filmanalyse
101 S., DIN A4, kart. Best.-Nr. 041228

Four Weddings and a Funeral
Filmanalyse
115 S., DIN A4, kart. Best.-Nr. 041178

An Inconvenient Truth
Filmanalyse
91 S., DIN A4, kart. Best.-Nr. 041186

Outsourced
Filmanalyse
110 S., DIN A4, kart. Best.-Nr. 041172

Slumdog Millionaire
Filmanalyse
90 S., DIN A4, kart. Best.-Nr. 041189

Don DeLillo: Falling Man
99 S., DIN A4, kart. Best.-Nr. 041181

Mark Haddon: The Curious Incident of the Dog in the Night-Time
99 S., DIN A4, kart. Best.-Nr. 041252

Mohsin Hamid: The Reluctant Fundamentalist
92 S., DIN A4, kart. Best.-Nr. 041171

Lorraine Hansberry: A Raisin in the Sun
98 S., DIN A4, kart. Best.-Nr. 041241

Nick Hornby: About a Boy
inkl. Filmanalyse
93 S., DIN A4, kart. Best.-Nr. 041245

Nick Hornby: Slam
123 S., DIN A4, kart. Best.-Nr. 041248

Aldous Huxley: Brave New World
93 S., DIN A4, kart. Best.-Nr. 041249

Hanif Kureishi: The Black Album
114 S., DIN A4, kart. Best.-Nr. 041179

Nick McDonell: Twelve
100 S., DIN A4, kart. Best.-Nr. 041194

Robert Swindells: Daz 4 Zoe
91 S., DIN A4, kart. Best.-Nr. 041170

Tennessee Williams: A Streetcar Named Desire
102 S., DIN A4, kart. Best.-Nr. 041238